A COMPLETE GUIDE TO MAKING AND ARRANGING
DRIED
FLOWERS

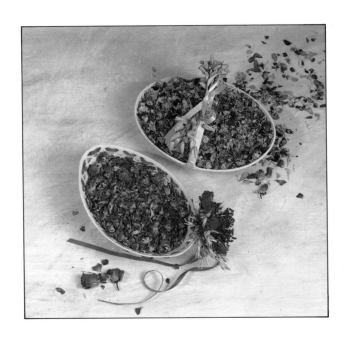

A COMPLETE GUIDE TO MAKING AND ARRANGING

DRIED FLOWERS

Susan Conder

GALLERY BOOKS
An Imprint of W. H. Smith Publishers Inc.
112 Madison Avenue
New York City 10016

Dedicated to the memory of Bernard Heller

The author would like to thank Neville, Gabby and Boo Conder for their patience and help during the development of this book.

Editor: Miranda Spicer
Art Editor: Caroline Dewing
Production: Craig Chubb
Picture Research: Moira McIlroy

Published by
GALLERY BOOKS
An imprint of W. H. Smith Publishers Inc.
112 Madison Avenue
New York New York 10016

ISBN 0-8317-2459-5

Typeset in Wales, U.K. by
Litho Link Limited

Printed and bound in Hong Kong by
Dai Nippon Printing Company

CONTENTS

Introduction	PAGE 10
AUTUMN	12
In the Shops	14
In the Garden	30
In the Wild	34
Techniques	39
Styles of Arrangement	44
WINTER	54
In the Shops	56
In the Garden	60
In the Wild	68
Techniques	71
Styles of Arrangement	82
SPRING	92
In the Shops	94
In the Garden	96
In the Wild	102
Techniques	104
Styles of Arrangement	112
SUMMER	120
In the Shops	122
In the Garden	124
In the Wild	127
Techniques	132
Styles of Arrangement	142
Glossary	150
Index	154
Acknowledgements	156

INTRODUCTION

The pursuit of a 'lifestyle' and the creation of a home environment which reflects that lifestyle is a prime activity in these relatively affluent times. A home that is restful, welcoming, attractive and uniquely personal is the ultimate goal of many people, ranging from young adults starting their first job and setting up house to retired couples enjoying their newly acquired free time. Visiting any large DIY centre or department store at the weekend confirms the intensity of this pursuit.

While some of the projects or purchases may be very expensive – and require planning, time and hard work as well as money – a bunch of dried flowers can fulfil the immediate impulse to improve the appearance of one's surroundings at a very modest cost. Dried flowers are the perfect medium for expressing creativity on the home front, because they combine beauty, economy, fashion and challenge. Dried flowers, like fresh ones, can be used with the greatest of Edwardian formality or with the informal exuberance of a child placing a fistful of newly picked flowers in a glass jar. Unlike fresh flowers, tightly packed dried flowers can cover an entire wall or ceiling with a textural surface of colour, like a *bas-relief* of blossom. On a smaller scale, a few sprigs of dried flowers can fill a tiny liqueur glass with a gem-like miniature display.

Unlike fresh flowers, whose lifespan is limited and whose immediate and continuous needs are exacting, dried flowers are long lasting and undemanding. Because dried flowers retain their beauty for months or even years rather than days, or at most, weeks, many people look upon them as an investment and can justify greater expenditure on dried flowers than on fresh. Secondly, but just as importantly, there is no pressure at the end of a busy day to 'deal with' a newly purchased bunch of dried flowers. There is no conditioning required and the flowers can be put on one side until more relaxed time is available.

Dried flowers are sometimes referred to as 'winter flowers' in old-fashioned books on flower arranging and as inferior substitutes for fresh flowers is how they firmly remain fixed in many people's minds. Although modern marketing techniques have done much to promote dried flowers all the year round, most books still tend to approach the subject with a bias towards winter. I have tried, in this book, to capture the rhythm and cycle of the dried flower year, giving equal weight to each season from the point of view of growing – gardening is, after all, another popular leisure activity – as well as harvesting, preserving and arranging. And although few readers are likely to participate in every aspect of dried flower cultivation, care, preservation and display, the separate pieces of information build up, like individual tiles in mosaic, to create the first complete picture of the world of dried flowers.

AUTUMN

Although the temperature drops in autumn, the autumnal palette is an increasingly warm, rich one. In the garden, the foliage of deciduous trees and shrubs provides a spectacular finish to the summer, turning yellow, orange, fiery red, russet and crimson. The flowers of autumn, especially dahlias, chrysanthemums and Michaelmas daisies, reinforce this richness, and even the cool, blue hydrangea may take on deep claret overtones as cold weather sets in. In the kitchen – more related to dried flower arranging than might first seem – feathered game makes its first appearance, together with all the gourds, grains, nuts and dried fruits. No season is as demanding as autumn in the yearly cycle of dealing with dried flowers. Much of the harvesting takes place now, of garden and wild flowers, seed pods, grasses, berries and fungi. Preserving such material, whether by air drying, desiccation or glycerining, follows directly on from collecting, and the two tasks flow together. A fine, dry autumn makes for a relaxed, enjoyable time outdoors, whether collecting material from the garden or from country or woodland walks. It also holds promise of a successful harvest, with material unmarred by storms and quick to dry. Autumnal rain or early frost sets up a challenge, a deadline against which to work and far from perfect conditions in which to do so. On the other hand, from inclement weather comes a special feeling of self satisfaction, once the flowers, pods and grasses are safely inside.

In the Shops

Dried flowers are now an accepted feature of most styles of interior design, and marketed with the same intense publicity and sales tactics as fresh flowers. Because dried flowers have a longer shelf life than fresh flowers and require no water, they are easier to accommodate in non-specialist stores. As well as the ordinary sources, gift shops and 'lifestyle'-type chain stores now feature dried flowers, a sure sign that they have 'arrived'.

Shops with a quick turn-over of stock, especially those directly connected to growers, are most likely to have freshly dried flowers. Sunlight quickly fades colour, so ideally, dried flowers should be displayed out of direct sunlight. Another tendency is for shops to create a solid wall of tightly packed dried flowers, in tiered shelving. This can look stunningly beautiful, but compacting the bunches can also break the stems and heads. (Those displayed at ground level are subject to accidental knocking.) Dried flowers displayed in the open air are subject to atmospheric moisture, as well as sunlight, although obviously, a country stall on a bright sunny day offers more promise than problems.

Making the Choice

Use your eyes to detect split bulrushes, missing florets from flower spikes, broken heads of fluffy, over-ripe centres of *Compositae* flowers, such as helichrysum. Grasses, too, that are over-ripe tend to have bits and pieces missing from the seed head. Gently tilting or shaking a bunch should reveal over-ripe or broken dried material. If you feel slightly guilty about assertive shopping, remember that flowers which fall apart in the shop would do so as soon as you unwrapped them at home. With material sold by the unit – bunches of bulrushes or roses, for example – a quick head count can help you select a full bunch.

Material sold in boxes, often with a cellophane window, is protected from dust and accidental knocking and, a certain amount, from sunlight, but you often pay extra for the

In some shops, dried flowers are displayed with the same creativity and sense of style as that found in homes. In other shops, more conventional racks or shelves are used. Whatever the presentation, a close inspection of potential purchases is always worthwhile.

packaging. Before buying boxed dried flowers, gently shake the box; if a snowstorm of debris floats past the cellophane window, chances are the material inside is over-ripe. And unless the material is boxed, ask the salesperson to wrap any dried flower purchases for you, including the top, to protect the flowers from weather and crowded pavements.

Pre-mixed bunches are popular. These can be composed of various colours of one species, such as statice or helichrysum; various plants in a single colour range, often cream, beige and tan; or a general mix of various colours and types. Although buying a mixed bunch is safe and may be the only option, particularly in smaller outlets, such bunches can sometimes look dull. (It is also a way that growers can dispose of slightly defective material or ends of lines.) Better to buy two: one pre-mixed, another of a strong single type, to give a particular character to a display.

Looking at a wholesale catalogue from dried flower growers or importers is almost like looking at a rainbow: page after page of dried flowers, in natural, bleached or dyed colours, ranging from white, cream, light yellow, dark yellow and orange through the spectrum to dark blue. Growers offer far more than any single shop can accommodate, and it may be possible to ask your florist to order specific material for you. Bunches are often sold in minimum numbers of five, however, so you may have to place a large order, or the florist might agree to sell the superfluous bunches that you do not want.

If any generalizations can be made, one is that natural dried flowers are often subtle rather than clear in hue. Even this, however, has its exceptions: the fierce tones of a mixed bunch of statice or helichrysum, for example. Another is that clear green is almost entirely absent from naturally dried material, although there are dyed green flowers and seed heads, usually of an olive, dun shade. Sometimes dried material is dyed grass green, to simulate fresh foliage, but it is usually unsuccessful, as it lacks the latter's variations in tone.

If you live in the country or visit for a country weekend, fêtes, charity bazaars and perhaps

garage sales at this time of the year yield treasures, both cultivated and picked wild. Material which is quite expensive to buy commercially – hydrangea heads, Chinese lanterns and pampas grass, for example – is often available for a fraction of the cost. Likewise unusual material, such as dried cornflowers, agapanthus and clematis seed heads, which are virtually unavailable commercially. Often there is mutual delight on both sides.

Buying Exotics

The same general rules for buying dried material grown locally, or in a similar climate to one's own, apply to dried exotics. What is exotic in one country may be commonplace in another, but in northern temperate climates, the vast majority of exotics come from South Africa and Australia.

The *Proteaceae* family provides a wealth of floral, fruiting and foliar material. The South African proteas and the closely related Australian banksias and dryandras are perhaps the most familiar. Each large protea 'flower' is actually composed of masses of tiny flowers surrounded by attractive, often hairy, petal-like bracts. Proteas come in an enormous range of colours and shapes, hence their name commemorates the ancient mythological god, Proteus, who had the ability to change his shape at will. They are also called Cape honey flower or Cape honeysuckle.

Banksia, or Australian honeysuckle, produces rather bottle-brush like flowers with colours ranging from greeny white to yellow, pink, orange and red, often with contrasting stamens; the similar-looking dryandras are available in the yellow and orange range. Sometimes the daisy-like calyces of *Protea nerifolia*, P. *compacta* and P. *repens* are sold under different names; and dried banksia foliage is sometimes sold separately. Other valuable, but rarer, members of *Proteaceae* include various *Leucodendron* species, whose flower-like bracts come in pink, gold, yellow or red, and whose spiky foliage dries well; and various species of *Hakea*, which provide attractive foliage, flowers and woody fruits. Lastly, the aptly named woody pear (*Xylomelum angustifolium*), carries hard, grey,

felted, inedible pear-shaped fruits in spring.

Other exotic seed pods include those of jacaranda, a Brazilian native that is widely grown in warmer climates. The pods, which are carried in clusters, look like tiny convoluted sculptures. They are rough, greeny brown outside, and inside are smooth and pale. Eucalyptus seed pods are also borne in clusters, and can be rounded, pear-, top-, or cup-shaped, according to species, often with a hollow centre. They are sometimes called bell cups in wholesale catalogues.

Although palms do grow in mild regions of North America and warm, coastal areas of Britain, especially areas favoured by the Gulf Stream, elsewhere they qualify as exotic. The elegant fronds of the sago palm (*Cycas revoluta*) or cycas palm, have been used decoratively for many generations, although often in funeral tributes. Freed of its mournful connotations, the sago provides excellent material for a modern, abstract display. Harvested commercially, the fronds are available in various lengths, and bleached or natural. Useful palms with fan-shaped fronds for sale dried, include the European fan palm (*Chamaerops humilis*) and the cabbage, or palmeto palm (*Sabal palmetto*). The latter's leaves can be up to 2.4m (8ft)

kangaroo paw

hakea

across, but can be cut to smaller sizes. Some are available dyed in brilliant or subtle colours. The date palms (*Phoenix* spp) provide broom-like flower sprays, and the rattan palms (*Calamus* spp), provide hanging clusters of dark-brown, acorn-like nuts.

Mail Order A maddening problem that occurs when searching through catalogues of imported exotics is that Linnaean names are usually replaced with common names of enormous inconsistency, or a bastardized version of the Linnaean name, sometimes combined with the native language of the importer. Calyces of *Protea repens*, for example, become 'Repens

supercut' in one catalogue. In another, bleached millet makes its appearance as 'Indian corn wit', a far cry from the traditional *Zea mays*, Indian corn, and 'wit' meaning 'white' in Dutch. Fortunately, most catalogues are heavily illustrated, so that the linguistic problem has a visual solution.

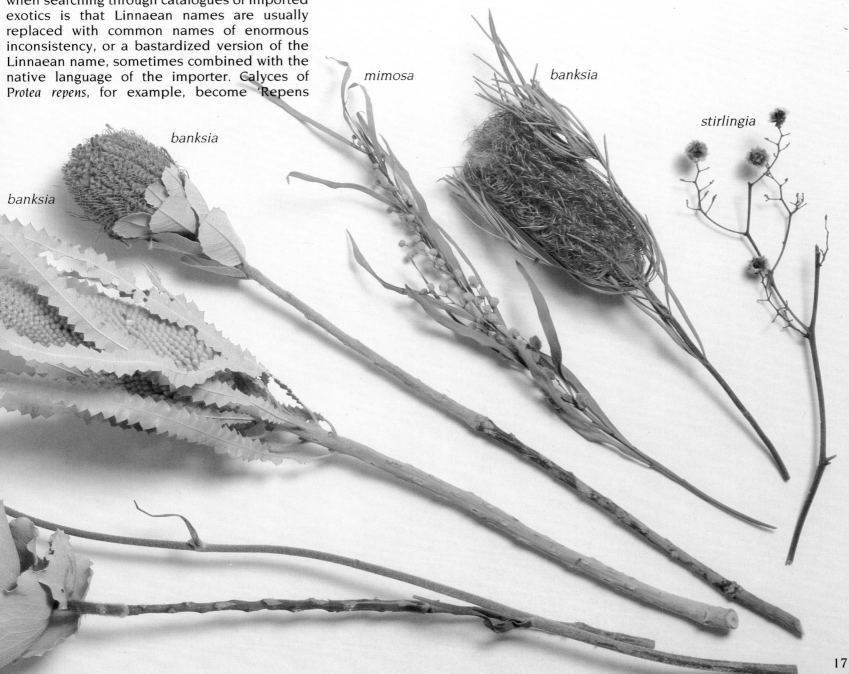

banksia

mimosa

banksia

stirlingia

banksia

banksia

17

mint

mugwort

stirlingia (dyed)

larkspur

chives

statice

rose bay willowherb

sea holly

hydrangea

cornflower

knapweed

hair grass (dyed)

echinops

heather

sweet William

love-in-a-mist

globe amaranth

helichrysum

xeranthemum

19

achillea (dyed)

florist's rose

anaphalis (dyed)

helichrysum

spiraea

sweet William

broom bloom (dyed)

hydrangea

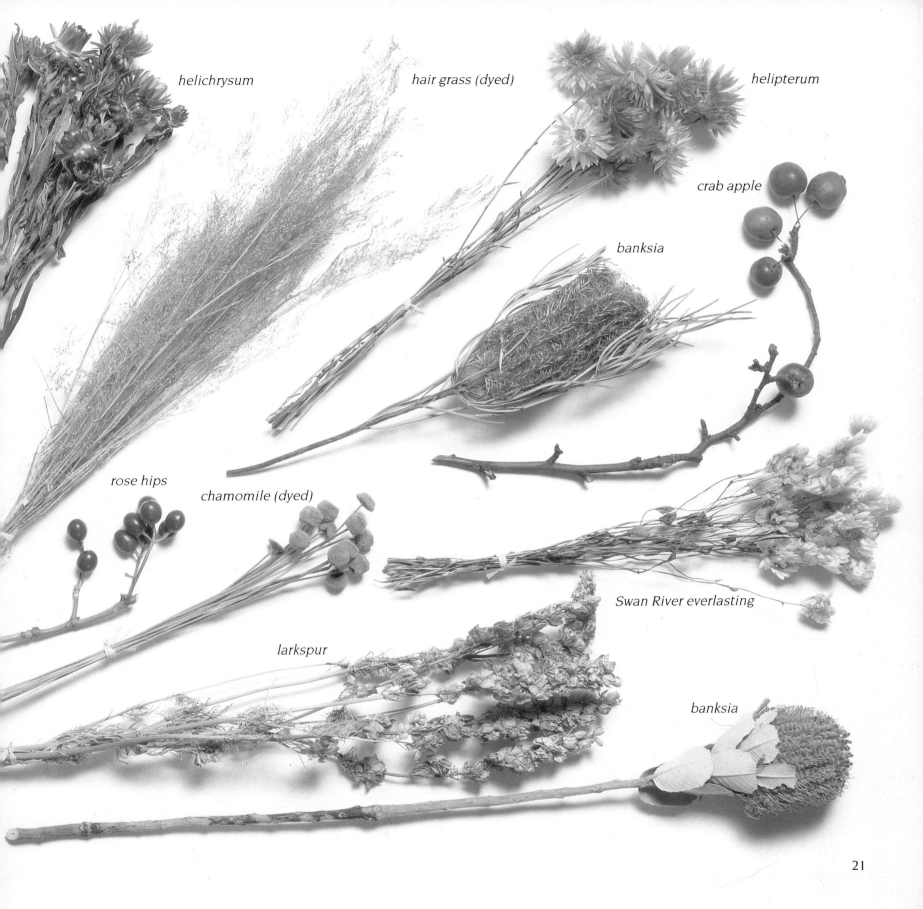

helichrysum

hair grass (dyed)

helipterum

crab apple

banksia

rose hips

chamomile (dyed)

Swan River everlasting

larkspur

banksia

21

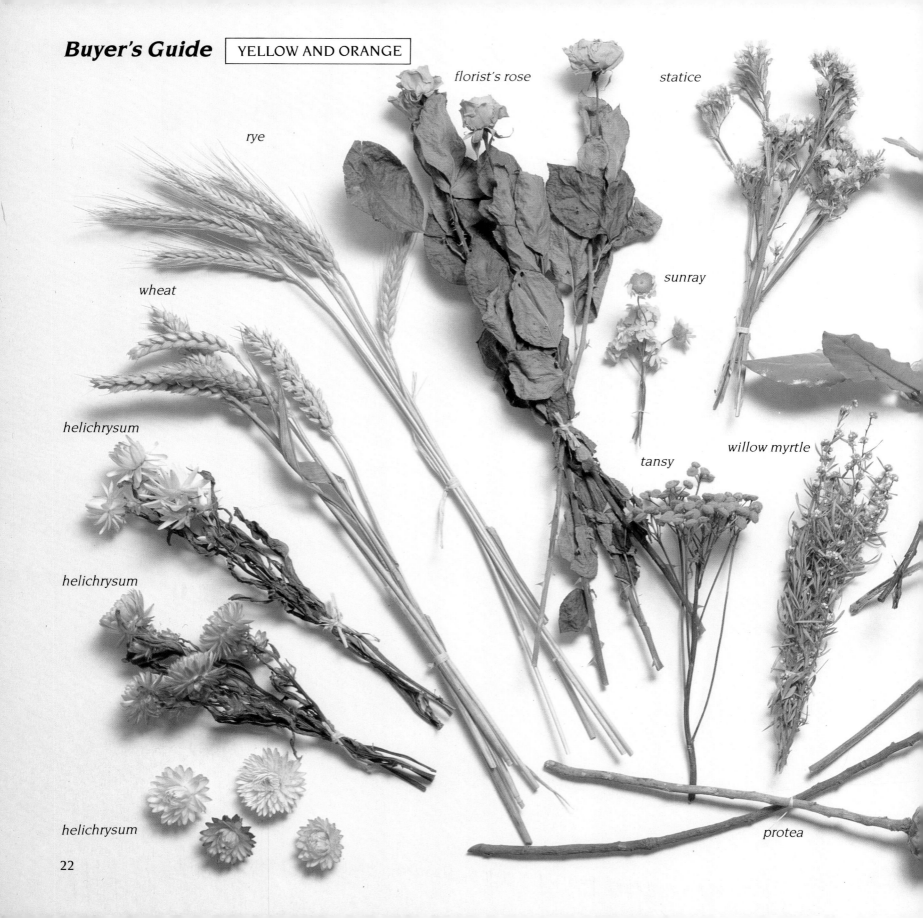

florist's rose

statice

rye

wheat

sunray

helichrysum

willow myrtle

tansy

helichrysum

helichrysum

protea

22

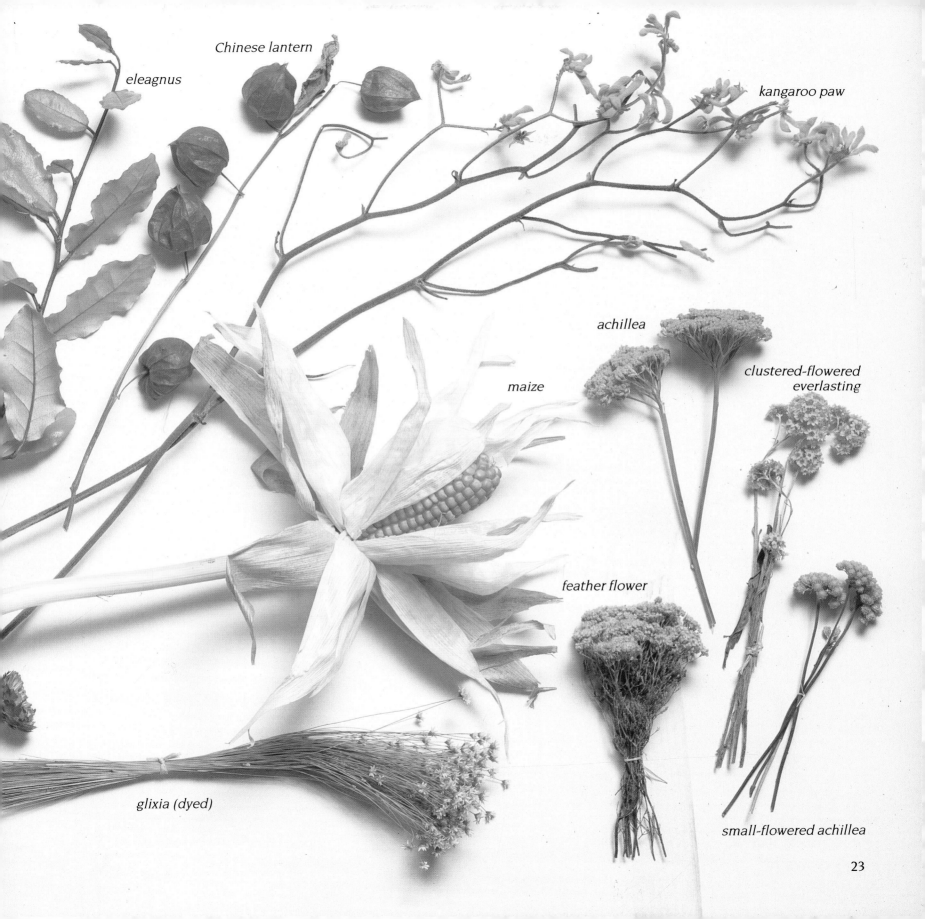

eleagnus

Chinese lantern

kangaroo paw

achillea

clustered-flowered
everlasting

maize

feather flower

glixia (dyed)

small-flowered achillea

23

Buyer's Guide GREEN

wheat

fern

timothy

broom bloom
(dyed)

safflower

quaking grass

hakea

banksia

love-lies-bleeding

canary grass

acanthus

hare's tail grass (dyed)

25

BROWN AND BEIGE

sweet chestnut

campanula

astilbe

annual scabious

dock

plantain

iris

26

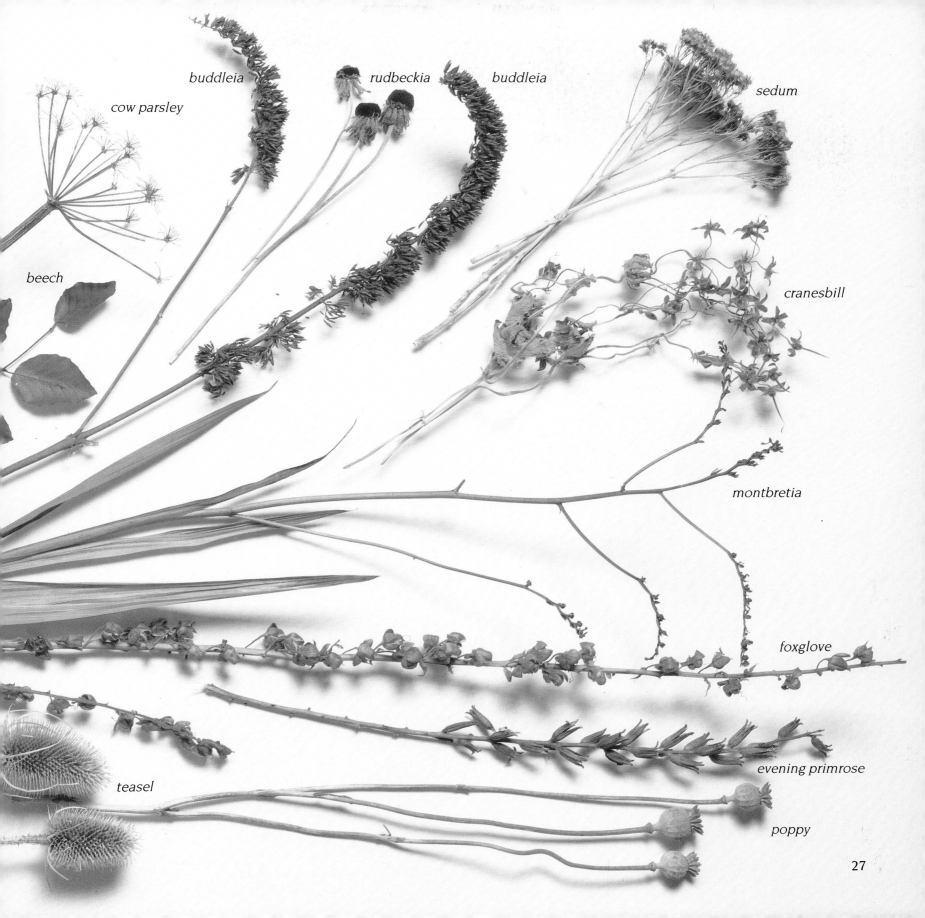

buddleia

cow parsley

rudbeckia

buddleia

sedum

beech

cranesbill

montbretia

foxglove

teasel

evening primrose

poppy

27

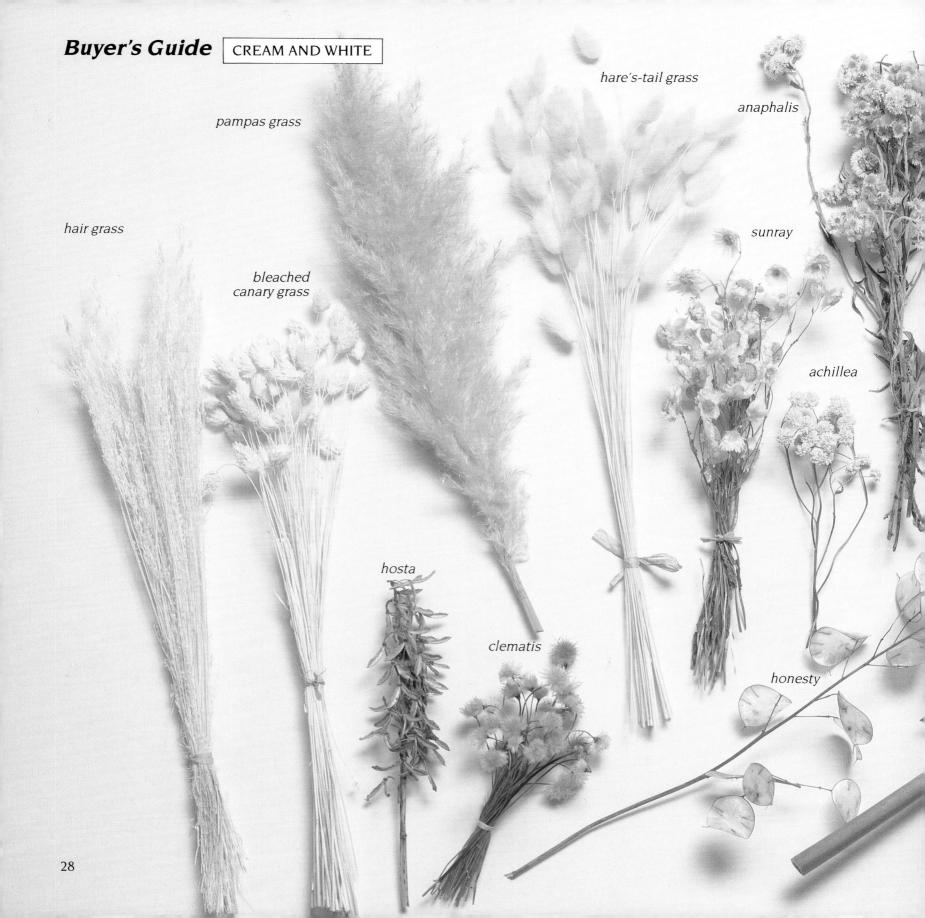

hare's-tail grass

pampas grass

anaphalis

hair grass

bleached
canary grass

sunray

achillea

hosta

clematis

honesty

grape hyacinth

clematis

leek

statice

xeranthemum

echinops

sea lavender

gypsophila

29

In the Garden

Although harvesting material for drying is traditionally thought of as an autumnal activity, it spans the other three seasons as well. Many herbaceous border perennials – delphiniums, paeonies, lady's mantle and astilbe, for example – peak in early summer. Mid- and late summer is the best time to harvest foliage for preserving in glycerine (see page 135-137), and pussy willow stems and catkin-laden alder, hazel and birch branches have a time table firmly rooted in the winter and early spring (see pages 67-70). The seed pods of species tulips, grape hyacinths, fritillaries and bluebells are harvested in late spring or early summer. The majority of plants – especially seed pods – for air drying, however, do tend to reach their optimum stage towards the beginning of autumn. Early-season herbaceous perennials sometimes produce a second crop of flowers then, too, especially if the main crop was cut before reaching its prime.

When to Harvest

Ideally, harvesting should take place after a long, dry spell, although not so dry that the flowers are wilting. Extended periods of rainy weather result in soft, succulent plant growth, which is difficult to preserve, shrinks excessively and often has a high proportion of foliage to flower. In cool temperature climates, timing a harvest is a question of balancing risks: the flowers and pods may need the last few weeks to open or ripen fully, but sudden frosts or autumn gales may ruin a whole year's work.

Make sure you have plenty of time immediately after harvesting to deal with all the freshly cut material. This is not as important for seed pods which have fully dried naturally, and only need storage, but material needing air drying, glycerining or preserving in a desiccant should be treated as soon as possible after being cut.

Harvest on a dry day. Wait until any dew clinging to the plants has evaporated, but avoid harvesting in hot, midday conditions, when flowers may be wilting, or in the evening, when dampness can settle in. Flowers to be dried in a desiccant are particularly liable to fail if picked during midday heat. Gently shake material to dislodge unseen insects, which can inflict damage later. If petals or leaves fall off, the material may well be overmature, although it could prove useful when collecting seed pods. Avoid flowers and foliage obviously damaged by insects, weather or disease, although one or two sub-standard, non-central blooms can often be removed from a composite flower head, and the remainder dried. In the case of foliage for drying or glycerining, thin out overcrowded foliage and remove awkwardly placed twigs or branchlets altogether.

Just as flowers for fresh arrangements can be picked at various stages of growth – in bud, just beginning to open, fully open, and in seed – to add interest to a display, some material for dried arrangements can be picked at different stages, from unripe bud to seed pod. The silvery buds of cornflower, for example, with just a touch of blue showing, are as useful as the fully opened flowers, and should never be discarded. (The seed heads that follow have their own merit, although blue is such a valuable colour it is a waste to grow cornflowers for the seed heads alone.) If you miss larkspur, paeonies or hollyhocks at the floral stage, you can harvest them at the seed-pod stage.

Other flowers have a very specific harvesting time. Flowers for preserving in desiccant must be cut in late bud or just before reaching their prime. Once pollen or seeds appear, the petals begin to fade and the join between them and the flower head weakens. Use this as a harvesting guide.

If material can be preserved by more than one method, the optimum time for harvesting can also depend on the method of preservation used. Fresh hydrangea blossom, when the tiny real flower in the centre of each flower-like bract is open, is suitable for preserving in a desiccant, to retain the clear blues, pinks and mauves. When these tiny flowers fade, the bract colour starts to deepen, fade or otherwise change, and the texture becomes thin and papery, the blossom can be air dried. (Air drying is an easier process and the resultant colours often have a subtle richness.)

Early autumn in a garden is often a more colourful and attractive time than late summer. The cooler, wetter conditions encourage many perennials and shrubs to put on a second display, and summer colours are joined by brilliant autumn foliage. Hydrangeas, invaluable for dried flower arranging, take on a papery appearance as the flower bracts begin drying naturally. Harvesting the flower heads now, and air drying them under cover, is safer than leaving them to the elements.

31

How to Harvest

As a general rule for daisy-like flowers, especially immortelles, harvest when you can see the centre but before the petals are fully open. The flowers continue to open while drying; if picked when fully open, the centres become over-ripe. If you want the centres alone, such as the black cones of rudbeckia or the yellow buttons of feverfew, pluck off the petals, or wait till they fade. Daisy-like flowers which are carried in clusters, such as ammobium and anaphalis, do not all open at the same time. Harvest when half to two-thirds of the flowers in a cluster are open. With helichrysum, you should just be able to see the yellow centre; if the yellow centre is fully visible when picked, it will continue ripening and become fluffy, and

Ammobium, or winged everlasting, below, and bulrush, right, can be disappointing if harvested when over-ripe. Harvest ammobium when two thirds of the flowers are open, and bulrushes when the tassel on the top of the stem comes into flower.

the petals curve backwards. Achillea and tansy, both petal-less *Compositae*, will not become fluffy when overmature, but their colour becomes heavy and dusty looking; pick just before they open fully.

Spiky flowers should generally be picked when the lower flowers are in full bloom and the uppermost flowers are still in bud; ideally, half the flowers in between should be open. Liatris, or blazing star, flowers from the top of the spike down; use the criteria in reverse. The spikes of love-lies-bleeding hang rather than spire, but they, too, should be picked when half the flowers are open. A genuine exception is rat's-tail statice, whose pinky purple spikes droop unless harvested when fully mature.

Flowers picked for their bracts should also be more mature. Harvest bells of Ireland when all the bells are open, but before the green colour starts to fade. The top flower buds of acanthus should be fully open, and the lower seeds just starting to form, but without any sign of fading on the bracts. Harvest the rounded bracts of phlomis as soon as the flowers fall.

Seed pods can be attractive when still green and closed, as in the case of campion; when partially open, as in the case of *Iris foetidissima* or when fully open, as in the case of milkweed, grape hyacinth and false indigo. Try harvesting the seed pods of a particular plant at several stages, if you are unsure. Keep notes of the results, for future reference.

Some seed heads are notoriously tricky: thistles, bulrush, clematis and pampas grass are ofted picked when they are fully fluffy, which is too late, and they shatter at the slightest touch. Pick clematis (and pasque flowers) as soon as the hairy whorls form; bulrush, when the tassels on the top of the stem are still in flower; pampas grass, when the plume starts to stick out from the top of the stem; and thistles when the central fluff just becomes visible. (With thistles, you can usually rectify mistakes, as their flowerless calyces are decorative in their own right.) Seeds not contained in cases – sorrel, for example – need very careful handling. The less mature – i.e. the greener – they are, the less likely to become dispersed.

If you are clearing a bed of annuals, fork over the soil when finished, removing all roots and any weeds that have managed to grow. If you are following the annuals with spring biennials, apply a good general fertilizer first. Some

annuals, such as Prince of Wales's feathers and love-in-a-mist, can be pulled up by their roots, and hung upside down to dry with their roots intact. It is a good idea to shake excess soil from the roots first.

Plant Material for Air Drying

Flowers Suitable for Air Drying
Acanthus
Achillea
Allium (flowers and seed heads)
Ammobium
Antirrhinum (seed heads)
Astilbe
Barley
Bells of Ireland
Bistort
Bittersweet (seed heads)
Bluebell (seed heads)
Borage
Buddleia (flowers and seed heads)
Bulrush
Burdock
Calendula (flowers and seed heads)
Campanula (seed heads)
Campion (seed heads)
Candytuft (seed heads)
Carrot, wild (flowers and seed heads)
Catananche
Chamomile
Chinese lantern
Chive
Clarkia (flowers and seed heads)
Clary
Clematis (seed heads)
Columbine (seed heads)
Coriander (seed heads)
Cornflower (flowers and seed heads)
Delphinium
Dill (seed heads)
Dock (seed heads)
Echinops (seed heads)
Evening primrose (seed heads)
Feverfew (flowers and seed heads)
Flax (seed heads)
Foxglove (seed heads)

French marigold
Fritillary (seed heads)
Goat's beard (seed heads)
Globe artichoke
Godetia (seed heads)
Goldenrod
Grape hyacinth (seed heads)
Ground elder
Grasses, various
Heather
Helichrysum
Helipterum
Hogweed
Hollyhock (flowers and seed heads)
Honesty (seed heads)
Hops (seed heads)
Hydrangea
Iris (seed heads)
Knapweed (flowers and seed heads)
Lady's mantle
Lamb's tongue
Larkspur (flowers and seed heads)
Lavender
Lavender cotton
Love in a mist (flowers and seed heads)
Lupin (seed heads)
Mallow (seed pods)
Marjoram, wild (seed heads)
Milkweed (seed heads)
Mint
Montbretia (seed heads)
Mugwort (seed heads)
Nipplewort (seed heads)
Oats (seed head)
Pampas grass
Peruvian lily (seed heads)
Plantain (seed heads)
Polygonum
Poppy (seed heads)

Protea
Rape (seed heads)
Rhubarb
Rudbeckia (seed heads)
Rose-bay willowherb
   (flowers and seed heads)
St John's wort (seed heads)
Sage (flowers and seed heads)
Scabious (seed heads)
Sea holly (seed heads)
Sedum
Sisyrinchium
Spiraea (flowers and seed heads)
Statice
Sumach (Seed heads)
Sweet William
Tansy
Teasel
Thistle
Veronica (flowers and seed heads)
Xeranthemum

Foliage Suitable for Air Drying
Artemisia
Aspidistra
Bamboo
Broom
Canna
Curtonus
Eucalyptus
Ferns
Helichrysum
Eucalyptus
Hosta
Magnolia
Monkey puzzle
Senecio 'Sunshine'
Viburnum rhytidophyllum
White poplar

*The Bhutan pine (*Pinus wallichiana*), above, produces elegantly elongated cones. It is unusual among pines in that it retains its lower branches, making it an attractive garden feature, if space allows.*

*The Korean fir (*Abies koreana*), right, carries its violet, upright cones from an early age. Its dense, prickly foliage is as useful in dried flower displays – though not quite as long lasting – as its cones.*

In the Wild

Autumn is a particularly fertile season for finding material for dried arrangements. In many cases, nature has done the job of drying for you, and it is simply a question of an observant eye, and enough storage space. Cones, seed pods, and other non-floral material should never be seen as 'second best' substitutes for flowers, or horticultural leftovers from the season before. A few cones and pods, like some flowers, are very plain, but many are visually strong enough to be used on their own, in modern or traditional displays. Combined with dried flowers, they add substance and an element of surprise.

Conifer Cones

Conifer cones need not come from the wild, and interesting ones can often be found in gardens and botanical gardens. (The latter can be an excellent source of material, provided you get permission for collecting the fallen cones first.) Very few people, however, have the space or inclination to include rare conifers in their own gardens for the sole purpose of supplying cones for dried arrangements. Commercially grown conifer plantations provide pine, larch, fir or other cones, for Christmas decorations and for the rest of the year as well.

Conifer cones combine an architectural and natural beauty. Their interlocking scales are a miracle of geometric precision, and yet cones always have a restful, informal quality to them. The scales of a conifer cone remain tightly closed while the seeds resting on them ripen, then open, often doubling the size of the cone, to disperse the seeds. (Seed dispersal is sometimes accompanied by a loud cracking or popping noise.) Cones also tend to close when wet, and open when dry.

Cones are basically brown but vary from the reddish orange immature cones of some spruces, to the nearly black cones of *Abies forrestii* and the young blue cones of the Bosnian pine (*Pinus leucodermis*). Some cones that have been exposed to the elements take on lovely silvery hues, like old cedar shingles; others darken with exposure, and it is worth collecting cones of various ages, for a wider palette.

Sizes vary, too, from the tiny cones of thuja, cupressus, hemlock, cryptomeria and redwood – the latter, ironically, as potentially mammoth a tree as its cones are small – to the enormous, elongated cones of the noble fir (*Abies procera*) and the sugar pine (*Pinus lambertiana*). Those of the latter can reach a length of 50cm (20in); unfortunately, this huge tree rarely carries cones outside its native western North American habitat. The bristlecone pine (*P. aristata*), and bristlecone fir (*Abies bracteata*), as their names suggest, have intriguing, twisted bristles on their cones.

Larch and deodar cedar cones have the delicacy and appearance of tiny wooden rose buds, and can be used on their own stems – particularly graceful in the case of larch – or wired onto artificial ones.

Most cones can be collected when fully ripe, although those of firs (*Abies* spp and cvs) should be collected when not quite open, as both the seeds and scales drop off, once the seeds are ripe. The one exception is the so-called Douglas fir (*Pseudotsuga menziesii*), whose cones remain intact when ripe.

If cones have mud or sticky pitch on them, wash with detergent, using a stiff brush to remove heavy deposits. After washing, or collecting from the wild in damp weather, dry thoroughly before use or storage. Place them in a single layer, either outside in the sun or over a radiator or night-store heater.

The foliage of some conifers – cryptomeria, cupressus and thuja, for example – is as useful as its small cones. Use the branches with cones and foliage intact; the material should dry naturally *in situ* and keep for at least a season.

Pods

The opened cases of beech mast, found beneath beech trees at this time of the year, form woody little four-petalled 'flowers', and can easily be wired for use singly or in clusters. Collect the soft, rounded fruits of the plane tree – called buttonwood in America – before they are fully ripe, and the pods of both sweet and horse chestnut, either shut or partly open to

Thistles, such as this Onopordum, *above, can be found in wild and cultivated forms. Members of the vastly huge and useful* Compositae *family, thistles are useful for providing a more stark contrast to garden flowers.*

(right) Hops is a resident of hedgerows as well as being grown commercially for flavouring beer and, in its golden-leaved form, as an ornamental climber. Make maximum use of its flexible, trailing stems to soften the rigidly upright appearance of most dried flowers.

reveal the shiny brown nuts inside. Acorns remain in their little cups if collected when not quite mature; so do hazel. If collected when fully ripe, they soon part company from their cups, but a spot of quick-drying glue can remedy the situation. Because all these are potentially attractive to insects, store them with mothballs or a few sprigs of dried artemisia, to discourage infestation.

Wild plants vary from locality to locality – sumach (*Rhus typhina*) and milkweed (*Asclepias tuberosa*), for example, are American wild plants but garden ones in Great Britain. The pyramidal, velvety maroon antler-shaped seed cases of sumach, together with their pale stems, make instant arrangements on their own, or excellent backbones for mixed displays. Wait until the leaves have fallen before harvesting.

The pitted fruit cases of magnolias, natives of China, Japan and North America, are an additional bonus to their flowers. The seeds are usually bright orange scarlet, the cases, deep brown. The sceptre-like cases can be oval, rounded, columnar or twisted, and appear singly or in clusters, upright or hanging.

The indian bean tree (*Catalpa bignonioides*) and foxglove tree (*Paulownia tomentosa*) grow wild in North America and are cultivated elsewhere. Both have foxglove-like flowers followed by

attractive seed pods, produced only in warm summers. Those of the indian bean tree are very long, slender and dark brown; those of the foxglove tree are oval and smaller, about 5cm (2in) long, and hang like clusters of grapes.

Many trees and shrubs of the pea (*Leguminosae*) family have attractive dried pods: robinia, mimosa, gleditsia and Judas tree, for example. Even wisteria, grown solely for the beauty of its flowers, follows these with pea-pod like seed capsules of silky grey-green. The attractive downy texture remains after the pod is dried.

Hops (*Humulus lupulus*) carries its lantern-like seed pods in autumn; harvest lengths of stem, and hang them along a wire or clothes line to dry. Use the same technique for old man's beard (*Clematis vitalba*), harvested before the whorls have gone fluffy. The rampant bittersweet (*Celastrus orbiculatus*) should be picked after leaf fall, but before the outer shells concealing the bright orange berries have fully opened. Bittersweet has stronger stems than hops and clematis, and can be used immediately for display, where it will dry *in situ*.

The tree of heaven (*Ailanthus glandulosa*) is often considered coarse and weedy, but its seed pods turn brilliant scarlet red when mature; each pod is shaped like a miniature propeller. The pendant, wing-like seed pods of hornbeam, maples and sycamore offer a graceful contrast to more erect dried material. Those of maple and sycamore are often richly coloured in early summer and, if harvested and dried then, retain much of the colour.

Particular plant and local weather conditions dictate if late summer is a better time to harvest than autumn. The colour of the material varies according to when it is collected. Teasels, milkweed and burdock can be collected when still green, towards the end of summer, or when silvery beige, in autumn. Sorrel, or dock (*Rumex acetosa*), has seeds which vary from reddish olive to rich, russet-brown and finally, deep brown, as the season progresses. The unmistakable rigid bulrush, or cat-tail (*Typha latifolia*), should be picked in mid or late summer, while the golden tassels are still in flower; otherwise it falls apart.

Wild foxglove (*Digitalis purpurea*) and mullein (*Verbascum* spp) provide tall spikes of seed heads; on a smaller scale, various species of the humble plantain have spikes of tightly packed seeds, best picked while still green. Nipplewort (*Lapsana communis*) produces seed heads of tiny, rounded baubles on much branched stems, and makes a pleasant (and free!) alternative to dried gypsophila.

Also useful are the various umbellifer seed heads – ranging from cow parsley and ground elder to the giant hogweed (*Heracleum sphondylium*). The latter can cause rashes and should be handled with gloves. It is worth the extra trouble, though, for its huge, hollow stem can be cut into sections and used as vertical accents for modern displays, or even as a container for smaller dried material. The seed head of wild carrot (*Daucus carota*) is shaped like a lacy globe; if picked when green, it retains its fresh colour.

The daisy family provides as much potential material from the wild as it does from the garden. The velvety yellow seed heads of tansy (*Tanacetum vulgare*), chamomile (*Anthemis nobile*) and feverfew (*Chrysanthemum parthenium*) make a more delicate alternative to the heavy-headed cultivated yarrow. Thistles are also members of *Compositae*, and, like daisies, have 'flowers' composed of many florets, growing in a closely packed, concentric pattern round a central eye of additional florets. As well as offering potential with their central florets intact, many thistles have star-like calyces of silvery sepals that remain after the seeds are dispersed. Particularly beautiful is the carline thistle (*Carlina vulgaris*), with its huge and fiercely spiny calyx.

Lastly, allowing seeds of dock, thistle, or other troublesome wild plants to shed in your garden is self defeating. In the wild, however, shaking a few seeds onto the ground near where the plant is found perpetuates the supply for next year.

Feathers

Fantasy flowers can be made from the soft back or breast feathers of pheasant, partridge, wood pigeon or chicken. The feathers are wired to form 'petals' round a centre of artificial stamens, then attached to a wire stem. Longer tail feathers can act as fantasy foliage, replacing spiky leaves of crocosmia, for example. If you live in a rural area, especially if you know people who shoot, such feathers are easier to come by than if you live in an urban one. A butcher should be able to provide you with game feathers, particularly if you are a regular customer. More exciting still are game fishing tackle catalogues. Such catalogues contain pages and pages listing various bird capes (breast feathers still attached to the skin). Although meant for fly tying, these feathers are equally suitable for making into flowers. As well as selling individual capes of chicken or pheasant cocks and hens, specialist catalogues offer feathers of partridge, ostrich, teal, blue jay, turkey and maribou turkey, woodcock, goose, grouse, jungle cock, guinea-fowl and mallard plus other, more exotic, ducks in various natural and dyed colours. Some suppliers also have special 'bargain' offers of good-quality capes, sold by the dozen, in mixed colours, or end of season 'jumble' ranges, excellent value for money. As with dyed dried flowers, some dyed feathers are more natural looking than others. Those dyed in fluorescent colours, while they may attract fish, are often visually awkward used in displays with natural-toned material.

Fungi

Unlike dried flowers, dried fungi do not have universal appeal. Some people find nothing attractive in their fluid, abstract shapes and delicate colours, and confine their appreciation of fungi to eating commercially grown white button mushrooms. Other people see wild mushrooms as exciting material for floral display, as well as a gourmet delicacy. (Much less care is needed in choosing those for display, than those for eating.)

Identification Walks through the woods at this time of the year should yield good specimens; from the beginning of September to the end of October, given warm temperature and adequate rain, is the best time to look. Bracket fungi, which grow on stumps or cantilevered out from the trunks of trees, are sometimes naturally rounded and can be dried and used as containers. Smaller bowl-shaped fungi such as *Clitocybe* and the delicious, orange chanterelle, *Cantharellus cibarius*, can be dried and used as flowers. For an unusual, sombre tone, dry the velvety black, funnel-shaped, horn of plenty (*Craterellus cornucopioides*). Found in clusters among dead leaves under beech, it has the appearance of an exotic flower. While it is still fresh, insert a stem of grass or other natural material into a 'flower' fungus; the fungus shrinks as it dries and fixes itself firmly onto the stem. Dry them over a slow, steady source of heat, such as an airing cupboard, radiator or night-store heater.

Flat and irregular-shaped fungi are useful for the base of an arrangement, to conceal its support. Some, such as the oyster fungus (*Pleurotus ostreatus*), found usually on beech, dry naturally; others dry best placed over a source of artificial heat, as above. Look at the undersides of the fungi as well as the upper surface; some, such as those of the genus *Ganoderma*, have attractive patterning on the gills, and can be displayed upside down. On elder, you can sometimes find Jew's ear (*Auricularia auricula*); it is a deep, rich brown bracket fungus and though gelatinous when moist, dries bone hard. The polysticus bracket fungus (*Trametes versicolor*) has beautiful concentric rings of colour on its upper surface – blue, black, silvery grey, green, yellow or brown. It also has an unpleasant smell when fresh; but this disappears completely once the fungus has been dried.

The polysticus bracket fungus (Trametes versicolor) below, *has concentric rings of colour on its upper surface. When dried, it can form the base of a display. Given a wire stem, it makes an unusual addition to autumnal arrangements, rather like flowers of the most exotic sort.*

A typical selection of dried fungi, below right, available from florists and from the wild. Dried fungi, such as sliced boletus, are also available from specialist food shops, but tend to be very expensive and not particularly attractive to look at.

Techniques

Dried flowers are fragile, but it is important to put this in perspective. Fresh flowers also need careful handling, so they are not crushed or bent; with fresh flowers, in addition, you are always working against the clock, and even quite short periods without water can be disastrous. Though artificial flowers of plastic, polyester and silk have virtually no risk of damage during handling, you pay for it in other ways – coarse stems and sometimes a general lack of delicacy.

Handling Dried Flowers

Unlike fresh flowers, dried flowers are expected to survive several re-arrangements, and perhaps being moved from one place to another, so a certain amount of fall-out is inevitable. Often it does not matter, and is simply a question of sweeping up a few dried gypsophila or lavender florets from the table or floor. Major breakages, such as a dried rose snapping at the head, can sometimes be repaired (see page 151), but prevention is better than cure.

Because they are brittle, the stems and heads of dried flowers do tend to snap rather than bend. (Glycerined material is more flexible and therefore less vulnerable.) Always handle dried material by the stem, never by the flower or seed head. Keep well away from the neck join between the flower and stem, which is the weakest part. Flowers preserved in silica gel are particularly brittle, and petals may shatter completely at the slightest knock. In the case of long-stemmed flower or seed spikes, touch only the lower, bare stem.

Be careful when inserting or extricating a single stem into or out of a densely packed arrangement, or adjacent plants in storage. Those with thorny stems – teasels and roses, for example – or intricate branching systems, such as gypsophila, are liable to become enmeshed with their neighbours and break off. Avoid using force, whether pushing or pulling. Snip out any tangle, with florist's scissors or secateurs, to limit the possibility of damage.

The lower down the branching occurs on a stem, the more difficult to insert it in a partially built up arrangement. Such stems are best placed in position early on, or some of the lower branches removed if that is not possible. Some dried material is a genuine menace – the worst offender is burdock, which attaches itself to plants and clothing with equal enthusiasm. Again, as it is much branched, and can form a natural framework for a display, it is usually easier to position it first, then work other material round it. (You could take the opposite approach, and beat burdock at its own game; stick stemless burdock heads directly onto arranged dried material, rather like sticking gummed shiny stars on paper!)

Although there are bound to be exceptions, as a general rule working from the heaviest material to the lightest minimizes damage. Having a smooth, clear work surface also helps, as does keeping material chosen for arranging, but not yet used, in cardboard boxes or large coffee tins. It is amazing how quickly an unruly heap of potential material can accumulate on a work surface.

If you can build up the arrangement, particularly if it is a large one, in its permanent position, you avoid the risk of damaging material in transit. Stems that appear firmly fixed but are just lightly resting in florist's foam can be dislodged by movement, and if they are heavy, can topple adjacent stems, with an unfortunate house-of-cards effect.

Air Drying

Air drying is the most natural (and inexpensive) method of preserving material. Some plants, such as honesty, sea holly and immortelles, dry well of their own accord, when they stop taking up water at the end of the growing season. However, many other flowers and seed pods need additional help to dry, to retain colour and prevent shrivelling. Drying indoors also eliminates the risk of foul weather ruining perfect material.

Air drying works best with material that has minimal sap and is as dry as possible to start with. A complete list of plants suitable for drying would run to thousands of entries, but

Though mixed dried flowers, above, make a lovely display hung upside down, they are actually best dried in separate bunches, each according to kind, right. This is because drying times can vary considerably, and some species may be ready long before others.

the list on page 33 is a good starting point. As a general rule, thistles and burrs, daisy-like plants, flower heads composed of many tiny flowers, particularly umbellifers and grasses, and plants with papery bracts, calyces or seed pods are worth trying.

Because the weather conditions vary from year to year, material grown in cool wet summers can be more difficult to air dry than that grown in hot dry ones; flowers or seed heads that have dried perfectly one year may be dismal failures the next, even though given exactly the same treatment. Think of this method as an art, rather than an exact science; unexpected failures are usually balanced with brilliant successes.

The atmosphere in which the material is to be dried should also be perfectly dry and reasonably warm, with plenty of ventilation, and protection from direct sunlight. Exposure to sunlight fades the colours, as does a long, drawn out drying time. The material should also be as clean as possible – dust and grease free. (Mice can sometimes be a problem, especially when drying grains!) Attics, spare bedrooms or large, ventilated cupboards are good spots for air drying; in kitchens, the steam rising from cookers counteracts the benefits of the warm air. Garden sheds, garages, basements and outbuildings may be fine, but not in damp, wet summers or autumns. Many people swear by airing cupboards, and they are certainly worth experimenting with if you have one.

Suspension Most material is hung upside down to dry, so the weight of the flower or seed pod pulls the stem straight and prevents drooping at the neck. There are many methods of supporting flowers while they dry. Suspending a wooden or plastic trellis from a ceiling to form a false ceiling is an attractive possibility. Large mesh wire netting stretched tightly on a frame or tied to overhead beams is also effective. Heavy gauge mesh, available from building suppliers, does not need stiffening. Wire mesh used for reinforcing concrete, made of thin bars welded together at about 15cm (6in) centres, is available in rolls or flat sheets. Allow for head room and a means of access to the flowers, perhaps via a step-ladder.

Other possibilities include old-fashioned clothes drying racks, which can be raised and lowered, retractable clothes lines, and dowels or broom handles suspended horizontally in single or several levels. Hanging two or three bunches of flowers on a wire coat hanger first conserves space. Always leave gaps between bunches, and between the bunches and the wall, if they are hung from nails, coat hooks etc.

Most stems should be stripped of leaves, as they prolong the drying time and add nothing to the finished display. Some foliage, such as that of cotton lavender and mimosa, is as attractive as the flowers, and dries equally well. (Remove any foliage from the base of the stems, where they are tied together, to prevent rotting.) Flowers such as helichrysum, gomphrena and helipterum, that are usually wired, can be wired before hanging or part-way through the drying process.

Make small bunches; large bunches do not allow air to circulate freely, and flowers in the centre may rot before they dry. Flowers in densely compact bunches can become squashed or damaged by adjacent flowers or stems – the flat heads of achillea are a case in point. Tangled stems are another risk with large bunches. Each bunch should contain one type of flower, as drying times may vary considerably. The stems should be roughly the same level, but having the flower heads at different levels can actually speed up the drying process.

Tie the bunches as tightly as possible with freezer ties, gardener's twine, raffia or rubber bands. The latter are particularly useful as the stems shrink in the drying process; if you use string, tie it tightly, and twice round the material, so it is self adjusting. Use another piece of twine or florist's wire to hook the bunch to its support. Hang large spikes, such as delphinium, mullein and bells of Ireland, upside down singly. Thick-stemmed, bushy-headed celosias, and much-branched plants, such as burdock, should also be hung singly.

Drying Upright Some material dries best right-way up. Chinese lanterns, for example, dry at unnatural angles if hung upside down and look odd. Simply hook one of the upper lanterns

Flowers and pods suspended from pot hooks in a country-style kitchen can be a feature even as they dry. Steam from cooking may prolong the drying process, but it is a compromise many people are prepared to make for the effect.

naturally at the end of the season may need little or no extra drying time; if their stems are stiff, simply store them upright in a dry place. Those that have already taken on beige tones do not benefit from dark conditions.

Timing The time taken to air dry varies according to the thickness and water content of the material, and the atmospheric moisture and temperature. Check from time to time, and re-tie any stems that have come loose as a result of shrinkage. Most flowers and pods dry within two or three weeks. When fully dry they feel light, crisp and papery to the touch, and the stems should snap easily.

Foliage

Although air drying is largely done with flowers and seed pods, some foliage will air dry if hung immediately after cutting in a dark, dry, well ventilated place. The dried foliage is brittle to the touch and should be handled with particular care. Hosta, magnolia and aspidistra foliage can also be dried in glycerine; the advantage of the latter is flexibility, the disadvantage is the cost. The monkey puzzle tree, with its contorted, rope-like branches, looks extraordinarily out of place in most gardens. Lengths of branch, however, can be shaped and air dried into wreaths, hearts or wonderful abstract shapes.

Aspidistra leaves which start to turn dark brown at the tip can disfigure a house plant, but can be cut off and hung upside down to dry. Both they and hostas often develop interesting twists and curves when air dried. Silver-leaved plants, such as artemisia, helichrysum, lamb's tongue and senecio, retain their silver hue when dry, and are very useful for adding bulk to a display.

Variations

Some material benefits from a small amount of water, say 2.5-5cm (1-2in) to keep it from wilting while it dries in air. Hydrangeas (at the end of the season, once they have started to dry out naturally), heather, florist's mimosa, and hosta leaves are suitable subjects. Do not replace the water as it becomes absorbed or evaporates. Lavender, achillea, proteas, bells of Ireland,

over a rack or clothes line. *Clematis vitalba*, hops and grape vines can be stretched along the length of a line or pole, to dry in natural loops and curves, and if you are using them to form the basis of a wreath you should form them into a circular shape to dry. Wild grasses can be dried upright, and the weight of the seed heads gives the stems a graceful curve. Grasses can also be dried flat, in a single layer on newspaper; turn the material over every few days, for even and thorough drying.

With some flowers, a combination works best. Leeks, astilbe and lady's mantle are best hung upside down for a few days, then finished off right-way up, to fully maintain the natural shape of the flower head.

Pods and berries that have started to dry

eucalyptus foliage and hosta seed heads can also be dried this way.

To shape broom, willow or other pliable stems, soak them overnight in water, then tie them to the desired shape, using a lampshade frame, for example, as a mould. Dry in an airing cupboard, above a night-store heater or radiator.

Storing Dried Flowers

Store dried flowers somewhere warm, dry, dust free, out of direct sunlight and where they are unlikely to get knocked over. A well insulated loft or guest bedroom is reasonable, but as for the drying process, garages, sheds and cellars are likely to be unsuitably damp in winter. Avoid overcrowding, as the heads or stems of tightly packed dried flowers can become inter-locked and damage one another. Try, too, to avoid dramatic fluctuations in temperature, which can lead to condensation. Except in the case of silica-gel preserved material, there should be plenty of ventilation, to prevent attacks of mildew.

Inserting the individual stems of flowers into blocks of florist's foam, so the heads are not touching, then storing in a large box, such as a hat box, is ideal for precious silica-gel dried blooms, but it takes up an enormous amount of room. You can also rest such flowers on crumpled tissue paper, in air-tight containers.

A more space-saving alternative, and fine for air-dried material, is to store flowers and foliage resting horizontally in long cardboard boxes, with layers of tissue paper between each layer. You can sometimes get these boxes from florists, or clothes shops, and depending on the dimensions of the box, it may fit under a bed. Although silica-gel dried material should be stored in airtight containers, those preserved by air drying or with glycerine need air circulation around them. If there are no air holes in the sides of the boxes, make some with a sharp knife.

Pack the flowers in bunches, according to kind, loosely overlapping each bunch and putting them head to toe, to make maximum use of space. Very precious or delicate bunches should be wrapped in tissue paper before being placed in the box. Large spikes, such as delphiniums, are best stored singly, rather than in bunches. Material, such as foliage and some seed heads and grasses, which is long stemmed and relatively flat, needs not be bunched, but can be built up in layers, with tissue or newspaper between each layer.

You can also store air-dried flowers in the same way that they were hung, upside down from rafters, if you have enough room. Slipping a cone of newspaper over the dried bunch will keep it dust free and unfaded. If the dried flowers form part of the interior decoration, then covering them with protective paper is self defeating, and a bit of dust and faded colour are a small price to pay for months of visual enjoyment.

You can also stand them upright in empty coffee jars or other wide-necked jars or cardboard boxes, resting a layer of newspaper over them to keep dust and light away. As with material stored by hanging, material in jars can be as decorative in storage as it is in use.

Insects are fond of dried flowers and foliage, so add a few moth balls or dried stems of aromatic wormwood to the storage containers or storage area. It is also a good idea to place a few crystals of silica gel in any closed storage container, to absorb any moisture in the container or remaining in the flowers themselves.

Avoid storing glycerined and air-dried material together, as the former sometimes 'weeps' glycerine, and bits of powdery debris from the dried material may adhere to the surface of the glycerined foliage, making it unsightly and harder to clean.

Mark clearly on the outside of closed containers what they contain, to avoid unnecessary ferreting through three or four boxes to find exactly what you want. If practical, layer the materials so that types you are likely to use most often are towards the top.

Go through your stored material occasionally, especially if you dry flowers and foliage on a regular annual basis, and discard any that are broken or otherwise damaged. Those that have faded can be sprayed, stored separately and put to good use in a variety of ways at Christmas time.

A dry shed, sun room or greenhouse can be used for drying flowers, though in bright sunlight a certain amount of fading may occur.

43

Styles of Arrangement

Formal

Formality is neither good nor bad in itself – contrary to the ramblings of various design, socialite and fashion gurus – but simply a set of 'recipes'. These recipes vary from culture to culture and from generation to generation, and govern anything from aspects of behaviour at particular occasions, to seating plans and the arrangement of silver, china and crystal on a table. In terms of flower arranging formal western styles differ from formal oriental styles and adhere to shapes and proportions traditionally set down for various categories: 'L-shaped', 'horizontal', 'diagonal', 'vertical', 'oval', 'round', 'triangular' and the S-shaped 'Hogarth curve'. The proportions govern the container as well as the flowers.

Formal flower arrangements can be any size, as long as the proportions are correct, and are usually precise in outline. They are also usually densely packed, rather than loose and airy. Formal flower displays often have a gradation of material, with delicate flowers, seed pods and grasses used towards the outer edge of the display, and larger, heavier material towards the centre. The largest flower or cluster of flowers often forms a central focal point, although focal points are not strictly necessary. Within the main categories, there are many variations: a crescent-shaped display, for example, can be upright, like a new moon; convex like a smile; or concave, like a frown. As with informal displays, formal arrangements can be designed to be viewed from one direction only, or in the round.

Formal floral displays can reinforce the formality of religious occasions, such as christenings and weddings; or social ones, such as balls or formal dinners. There also seems to be a trend towards using informally arranged flowers at private formal occasions. This trend has acquired a reverse snob appeal rather like Marie Antoinette playing shepherdess.

Autumn is the season for exuberance and generosity with dried flower displays. In many cases, 'flower' is a misnomer, as seed pods, foliage, berries, cones, feathers and even oak galls offer a rich enough palette.

Using Dried Flowers Formally

Dried flowers are easier and more difficult to use formally than fresh flowers. The straight stems of dried flowers reflect the geometry of formal displays, and once positioned, do not wilt, twist or flop, as fresh material sometimes does. For new or hesitant flower arrangers, it simply becomes an exercise in choosing a shape, then filling it in, rather like filling in a colouring book outline, in three dimensions instead of two.

On the minus side, the straight, leafless stems are unattractive, and dried flowers, with their potentially static quality, can appear particularly lifeless when arranged in a predictable, geometric fashion. Ample use of filler material, such as dried gypsophila, nipplewort, lady's mantle, broom bloom or sea lavender, can conceal or disguise the stems. (Using seried ranks of flowers to conceal stems is another alternative, but this can be very heavy looking as well as expensive.) And within the formal framework, there is also room for ingenuity and experimentation. You may prefer a traditional formal display with comfortably toning colours and well-loved flowers, such as dried pink roses, pink delphinium and white gypsophila. But unexpected colour combinations, an unusual choice of material or both can enliven and personalize a formal arrangement. Dried chamomile, bistort and chive flower heads, for example, would make a charmingly original formal centrepiece in the round. And a display of near-black rudbeckia seed heads, dried crimson sumach heads and blue grey eucalptus leaves would be exciting, however banal the geometry.

Harvest Displays

Harvest festivals in churches, and the American Thanksgiving, incorporate a joyous mixture of gratefulness, praise, food and family celebrations. Floral displays are an inherent part of both these festivals, and dried flowers have the triple advantage of particular seasonal relevance, longevity and the rich autumnal tones that one associates with these festivities. It is also the one time of year to look at food – more specifically, raw or dried ingredients – with an

Chinese lanterns, above, are one of the staple ingredients of autumnal displays. Try drying a few while the pods are still green, as green is always a welcome colour in dried flower displays and, in many ways, easier to use than orange.

A harvest arrangement, left, combines ripe grain, maize, Chinese lanterns, dried bracket fungi and sweet chestnuts. The latter are supported by stub wires, concealed in the hollow stems cut from the grain. (Never throw anything away!)

47

Turk's cap gourds, above, are among the most spectacular of autumn produce. Display them singly or in groups, and surrounded with flowers or as a base for an arrangement.

A more sophisticated alternative to a carved pumpkin, this Hallowe'en display, right, uses a Turk's cap gourd as the base. A small block of florist's foam is impaled on a florist's frog, held in place with mastic, on top of the gourd. Into this foam is stuck a dense mass of love-in-a-mist seed pods, achillea, quaking grass and fresh kumquats, supported on stub wires. The kumquats last at least a week, and can be replaced with fresh, if required. Cork oak bark, available from tropical aquarium shops, forms an unusual base for a collection of edible squashes.

imaginative eye, and try to incorporate it into decorative displays.

Using Gourds These are usually dried for harvest displays (see pages 109-110), but there are several ways to cheat. You can use smaller ones fresh, simply piled into a wide, shallow bowl edged with a ruff of tightly packed dried flowers and seed pods. Either tuck the flowers into the interstices between the gourds, or use an outer florist's foam wreath as a base. Or reverse the roles and have a tall, arching rounded display of dried flowers and seed pods, with an edging of small gourds.

Gourds can be held in position on a table with dabs of florist's mastic or ordinary mastic, or wired, using medium-gauge stub wires, and inserted into a moss-covered florist's foam wreath. Push the wire through the base or side of the gourd, depending on which is its 'fair face' and when the wire is equal on both sides, bring the two pieces together and twist to make a stem for mounting. You may need a heated skewer or metal knitting needle to pierce the skin. If you do wire up gourds, they are shorter lived than those left whole. Some people prefer to glue very small gourds to golf tees instead, then insert the tees into florist's foam.

Use fresh gourds, either ornamental or edible, as containers for dried flowers, foliage, grains or seed pods. Chop off the top, hollow out the seeds, then insert a suitably-shaped piece of florist's foam, wrapped round the sides with cling film to prevent moisture reaching the stems of the dried material. One huge pumpkin could sprout a fountain of berry-laden hawthorn branches, dried grain and dried flowers, as a more sophisticated alternative to a carved jack-o'-lantern for a dining-table centrepiece. Crab-apple branches, stripped of foliage but with the fruit intact, would be a handsome alternative; both hawthorn and crab apple last several days out of water, though the fruits eventually do shrivel. Tiny, flower-filled gourds could decorate each place setting. For a shorter-term display, carve the centre out of fresh aubergines, apples, or pears, pack the cavity with florist's foam as described above, and make an arrangement with a selection of dried flowers.

49

Grain From ornamental Indian maize to wheat, oat and barley, grains are quintessential harvest symbols. (Stalks of millet, with their elongated tightly packed heads, can be had quite inexpensively from pet stores, where it is sold as bird food!) Instead of a grain sheaf, try making a field of grain in miniature, by packing shortened stalks vertically into a shallow square or rectangular box of florist's foam. Conceal the edges of the foam with dried sphagnum moss or ribbons. And instead of the familiar swag of Indian corn, try a little forest of upright Indian corn 'trees', each drilled to receive one end of a wooden dowel, the other end of which is inserted into a moss-covered florist's foam base.

A wooden decoy, right and far right, sits in his nest of dried grasses, sea lavender, hydrangea, helichrysum, statice and thistle. A circle of raffia forms the base, on which the more decorative material rests. When building up a display in situ, do not worry about permanent stability; using gravity is easier than wiring, and in the majority of cases, just as effective.

Mock game Game – duck, pheasant, turkey and hare – is another harvest image, although decorating with game itself is largely out of favour. Nonetheless, making dried flower and grain 'nests' for painted, wooden decoy ducks captures the spirit of autumn with none of the morbidity. For a long, narrow, dining-room table, a row of 'nesting' ducks would make a superb linear centrepiece. Sporting goods shops have expensive wooden decoys and less expensive plastic ones. Brilliant or rich brown game tail feathers can add vertical touches to an autumnal display.

Pulses and Sweetmeats Food shops, particularly health-food shops, offer rich supplies for a poetical, rather than literal, interpretation of harvest festivities. Dried pulses, in every colour from white haricots to orange lentils and red kidney beans, can be used to line glass containers filled with florist's foam. Although ropes of dried dates, and rich dried apricots, pears, peaches and prunes, are lovely for harvest decoration, mixing these slightly sticky fruits with dried flowers leads to unpleasant eating. The Victorians had the right idea, with their tiered epergnes: use an old-fashioned tiered cake stand, alternating layers of fruit and dried flowers. Nuts in their shells and dried flowers are compatible, and a wicker basket of nuts with a rim and handle of dried flowers would be most attractive. Try to include a few filberts or hazels in their ruffled coverings, or sweet chestnuts in their prickly green ones for contrast and variety.

A pewter mug, old wooden pull toy and patchwork quilt set the muted tones for this Colonial display. A mixture of dried herbs, rose hips and berries, old-fashioned garden flowers and wild flowers are presented informally. There is no hint of contrivance or 'art', though, in fact, such arrangements can take some time to perfect.

Colonial Style

America is proud of its Colonial past, and everything, from new kitchen units and housing developments to shopping malls, are given neo-Colonial overtones, in the same way that the British equivalents are given neo-Georgian ones. With dried flowers, however, it is possible to recreate an authentic historical style, using the same types and combinations of flowers as originally used, and similar containers, whether reproduction or genuine.

Puritan Early American Colonial style is associated with New England and, in the case of domestic arts and crafts, with a functional, Puritan sparseness and beauty. There was little leisure time available, so flower arrangements, as described in contemporary books, were simple. Gardens were given over to vegetables, fruits, herbs, medicinal crops and dyes, although some pot and medicinal crops, such as hollyhocks, roses, paeonies, and marigolds, had ornamental value as well. There were also wild grasses and flowers, such as rudbeckia, or black-eyed Susan; goldenrod; tansy; yarrow; cow parsley, or Queen Anne's lace; sea lavender and sumach. Wild berries and pods included teasel, dock and bittersweet, or celastrum.

Informal mixtures of dried wild and garden flowers, grains, grasses, seed pods and herbs were typical, gathered and displayed as if the bunch were simply transferred from the hand to the container. Dried foliage was not featured, nor was there any specific focal point. Instead, there was a texture of pods, flowers and berries, evenly built up from a central point and reminiscent of autumnal fields and gardens. Containers were usually kitchen utensils, such as woven baskets; simple brass, pewter or copper bowls, pans or tankards; or stoneware or ceramic jugs.

'Georgian Colonial' As America became financially more secure, the urge for the finer things of life became apparant. Williamsburg, Virginia, with its strong ties to England, mirrored the finest English Georgian style; this period in America is sometimes called Georgian Colonial. There was more time and space for ornamental flower gardens, and a great many new plants were imported from Europe. Flowers for drying were harvested and bunched in autumn for use during the winter months.

Flowers were now displayed in dense, formal masses, usually portrait or landscape proportion rather than circular. Two or three large flowers often formed a focal point, with more delicate, lacy material as a soft outline. There was a more sophisticated approach to colours, with pastel hues; rich, deep hues; or monochromatic themes, of every shade of blue or pink, for example. Instead of kitchen utensils, ornamental vases, often imported from England, France, Holland or China, were used. These included cut-glass tumblers; English creamware, such as five-fingered vases, which displayed the flowers in a fanned-out form; Dutch blue and white enamelled vases; and blue and white Chinese export porcelain ware. Some containers were perforated, to hold the flower stems, and others had spouts. The flower displays of Georgian Colonial America had equally formal and elegant settings, but simple backgrounds form an effective contrast.

American Eighteenth Century Flowers
The following, suitable for drying or preserving in desiccant, are some of the flowers mentioned in contemporary publications.

Amaranthus	Dictamnus	Pansy
Anaphalis	Globe amaranth	Pink
Artemisia	Globe thistle	Poppy
Asphodel	Goldenrod	Pulsatilla
Auricula	Grape hyacinth	Rose campion (Lychnis)
Bachelor's buttons (cornflower)	Hollyhock	St John's wort
Balm of Gilead (probably lemon balm)	Honesty	Sea lavender
Bee balm (Monarda)	Horned poppy	Solomon's seal
Broom	Iris	Straw flower (Helichrysum)
Candytuft	Larkspur	Sweet scabious
Calendula	Lily	Sweet William
Canterbury bell	Love-in-a-mist	Sweet sultan (Centaurea)
Clematis	Lupin	Tree mallow
Cockscomb	Marigold, African	Veronica
Columbine	Marigold, French	Violet
Everlasting pea	Molly allium (Allium moly)	Zinnia
Foxglove	Paeony	

WINTER

During the winter months, tree and shrub branches, overlooked during more verdant seasons as simply structural support for flowers and foliage, are seen with fresh eyes. Branches that 'all look the same' the rest of the year suddenly take on individual character. Leafless birch is lacy; beech is slender and elegant; each stumpy oak branchlet looks like an oak tree in miniature; and alder, with its male catkins and lantern-like female cones, looks distinctly oriental. Brightly coloured dogwood; lichen-covered oak and apple; and curiously contorted willow and hazel, make their way into dried flower displays, or become decorative displays in their own right.

Winter is also the season for cones – not just metallic-sprayed ones at Christmas, but big bowls of mixed cones, set out like fruit on a table; cone-covered, leafless branches of larch displayed generously and informally; and cones, such as cryptomeria or even pine, used in the natural setting of their own foliage. Most conifer foliage is long lived out of water, and to exclude it from dried flower displays or books on dried flowers because it is neither dried nor floral, is very limiting.

Christmas calls for special ingenuity, for presents to be made and decorated, and for the home to be filled with visible signs of warmth and hospitality. Dried material is valuable for all of these pursuits, from the most lavish gift bouquet to the humblest flower head, glued to the trailing end of a ribbon bow.

In the Shops

The great thing about containers for dried flowers is that so few are actually unsuitable. Unlike containers for fresh flowers, those for dried flowers need not be watertight, or have rims for holding water. They need not be any particular colour, size, material or proportion, as long as they are in keeping with the mood and style of the flowers they contain; and of your home, especially the immediate surroundings in which they appear. In fact, you probably already have more than enough containers or potential containers in your living-room, dining-room, kitchen, bathroom and garden. The need for new acquisitions is a primordial and powerful one, though; finding and working with new or unusual containers is a pleasant challenge, and prevents displays becoming repetitive.

Choosing Containers
Look for modestly priced containers in oriental shops, kitchen shops and cookware departments of large stores, garden centres, basketware shops, junk shops, garage sales and the bric-a-brac stalls of charity fairs. At the expensive end of the market, there are antique shops, auctions and art galleries, as well as shops selling fine china. Shops in larger museums often have quite good reproductions of vases in their collection at reasonable prices. As a general rule, buying two identical containers gives more scope for creativity than 'one-offs'. Also useful are containers identical except for size: large and small white-glazed soufflé dishes, for example, or pint and half-pint glazed stoneware mugs. Ironically, florist's shops make poor hunting grounds, as they are often limited to white plastic containers, or china vases heavily decorated with painted or transfer-printed flowers.

Taste in containers is personal, and your own instincts are as good a reference point as any. If a container elicits the spoken or unspoken response, 'I don't really like it, but it's such a bargain', or 'I can probably hide the worst bits

with flowers', look for an alternative. It is very easy to have a good range of fashionable containers, as there are several high street chain stores which declare what is fashionable as well as sell it, at eminently affordable prices. What is stylish or fashionable does not necessarily stand the test of time, though, as a glance through old magazines and books proves. Many aesthetic critics feel that appalling taste was rampant during the latter decades of Queen Victoria's reign; and even the rekindled interest in all things Victorian cannot overcome the general dislike for the over-ornate, over-decorated and contorted vases manufactured then. Today, it is unwise to spend a lot of money on jokey containers – teapots with feet on them, for example – as the joke soon wears off once you live with it.

Containers of any solid colour, except perhaps the disconcerting 'day-glo', light-reflective ones, are potentially suitable. White, black, and shades of beige and grey are always useful because they are neutral, providing a comfortable and non-competitive backdrop for dried flowers. (The beiges, creams and greys of natural stoneware, wickerwork and wood are particularly empathetic to undyed dried materials.) Pastel colours can complement the pale colours of dried delphinium, paeony, and the paler shades of helichrysum and statice, for example, or tone down more fiercely coloured blooms. Bright primary and secondary colours can complement dyed or naturally bright material; or add guts to a 'pretty-pretty' bouquet.

Choosing the same colour of flowers and container may or may not be a success. There are hundreds of shades of red, for example, ranging from red bordering on orange to red bordering on violet, and a 'near miss' between flowers and container may set up a jarring clash. Also, red-glazed porcelain, red-dyed plastic and red-sprayed wickerwork have different light-reflective qualities and connotations, even if the exact same hue is used.

A multi-coloured container can enhance or confuse a dried flower display, depending on the stridency of the pattern. Small, all-over patterns in harmonious or closely related colours tend to appear as a single tone: the so-

Containers made of natural materials, right, include stoneware and earthenware pottery and woven baskets of all descriptions. The latter have recently made the transition from modest utilitarian items to fashionable and often expensive symbols of good taste. For the best value, look for baskets in oriental shops, farm shops, junk shops and hardware stores.

Like dried seed pods, woven wicker baskets have a subtle range of natural colours, and 'multi-coloured' baskets, such as this one, can be quite charming.

called 'fly-speck' wallpapers are an example. Tiny checks or stripes are also 'non-invasive', and unless seen up close, blend into one tone. Such containers accommodate dried flowers without distracting attention from them. Once a pattern becomes 'readable', such as the traditional blue willow pattern, the dried flowers should have sufficient presence to take priority over their container. (It is better to leave an exquisite container empty than to fill it with unworthy flowers.) Containers decorated with very large patterns, and especially with representational pictures, need careful thought. Often the best solution is a huge floating mass of dried gypsophila, or monotone dried grasses: both magnificent in scale, but not competing with the container for close inspection.

Almost every raw material has potential, provided that the shape and decoration of the finished container are not awkward or over-fussy. Polished copper and brass have visual warmth, and their highly reflective sheen complements the matt quality and subdued natural colours of dried material. Silver and pewter are cooler in feeling, the former tending towards elegance and the latter tending towards unpretentious domesticity. Stoneware, terra cotta, china and porcelain are good, each in its own way: terra cotta flower pots are ideal bases for sturdy, dried flower 'trees', while fine porcelain is worthy of a display of rare and beautiful dried garden roses.

For a formal party table display, unused serving bowls or coffee cups and saucers matching the dinner service can be filled with dried flowers, as a large central feature or one at each place setting. Save any saucers that remain after cups are broken in normal household wear and tear. Fitted with florist's foam, the saucers make excellent bases for place setting displays.

Woven rush, wickerwork and bamboo containers are part of the same language as dried flowers, being dried plant material themselves, and are naturally compatible. With loosely woven containers, there is an added advantage: stems can be pushed in between the weave, to soften the slightly explosive effect of rigid stems radiating out from the top. When

buying wickerwork, do not just look in the kitchen department: an old wicker baby bassinet or crib on legs would make a good focal point, filled with dried flowers. On a smaller scale, so would a soft, wickerwork shopping basket, filled with dried flowers and hung on a wall; or a gingham-lined sewing basket. Even upturned straw boaters or floppy sun hats can serve as containers.

Transparent glass is the main anathema to traditional dried-flower arrangers, because the shrivelled, leafless, wired, crossed, poker-straight or otherwise unattractive stems are on view, together with any florist's foam or wire netting. Glass should not be discounted, however, as it can be lined with potpourri, reindeer or sphagnum moss, marbles or chippings. You can also treat the transparency as a challenge, particularly as no water is involved. In a wide-necked glass cylinder, begin building up the dried flowers well beneath the rim, with lower flowers concealing the stems of taller ones behind them. (You will probably have to construct the display outside the container, then carefully lower it into position.) Or make a simple grouping of branches, such as alder, dogwood or willow, which are attractive throughout their length, and need no camouflage. Decapitated dried flower heads can be stored and displayed at the same time, in old-fashioned lidded glass storage jars. And though not technically containers, round glass cake or cheese covers protect dried arrangements from dust and accidental knocking as well as adding a nostalgic touch, reminiscent of the Victorian bell jars.

Cut glass reflects more light than smooth-surfaced glass, and fragments the image of whatever it contains, so it does not clearly reveal awkward stems or florist's foam. Cut glass has such a hard character and wealth of intricate detail, however, that many people find that using cut glass with dried flowers is unfair to both. Engraved glass, unless it is heavily engraved, merely adds visual confusion to the problem of transparency, and is usually better avoided. Richly coloured glass in a single hue, such as American cranberry glass, or English blue Bristol glass, will effectively conceal the mass of unsightly stems in the container.

The size of useful containers ranges from tiny perfume bottles, medicine bottles or egg cups, to enormous soup tureens, milk churns, coal scuttles or even massive garden urns. Again, match the size to its setting; there should be some free space around a display, for visual effect and for the well-being of the flowers. Too much free space, though, and the display looks lost. The transition between a dramatic setting and a lonely looking one is subtle, and usually a question of trial and error, rather than mathematical rules. Sometimes the surroundings themselves act like containers: an empty fireplace, with crumpled wire mesh netting filling the grate, provides an excellent setting for dried flowers.

Matching the size of the container to the quantity of dried material is equally important. Some displays, particularly oriental or contemporary ones, do depend on a few, perfect specimens, but the general rule should be one of generosity. If an arrangement looks meagre in its container, and there is no more dried material available, try transferring it to a slightly smaller container of the same general shape. There may be minor adjustments to make, but the finished effect is usually more pleasing and better balanced.

The proportions of a container – its overall shape – are a matter of stability as well as taste. Traditionally, round or oval containers were meant to hold rounded displays of flowers, and tall thin containers to hold vertical displays. Today, virtually anything goes, and a rounded mass of love-in-a-mist can 'spill' out of a tall cylinder, or a forest of rigid-stemmed carthamnus grow from a perfectly round bowl. The taller and thinner a container, however, the more liable it is to topple over, especially as the weight normally supplied by water is absent. (Pebbles, gravel, marble or dried beans can be substituted.) The wider a container in proportion to its height, the stabler it is, but those with very wide necks as well as wide bases demand a large amount of dried material to look generously full. Gravy boats are usually a good shape for flower arranging: wide necked, stable, but not too large.

Containers with very narrow necks, such as wine bottles and pinched-in vases, are difficult to use, because dried flower stems simply poke rigidly upwards. You can glue a small, upturned jar lid to a cork slightly sticking out of a wine bottle, then fix a good-sized piece of florist's foam to the lid, using mastic and florist's spikes. (In an emergency, simply impale florist's foam on a florist's spike, fixed to the cork with mastic. It needs careful handling.) A straight-sided, narrow-necked container is easier; simply cut the florist's foam so that it stands above the rim. You can then angle the flower stems loosely outwards and downwards as well as upwards. If the arrangement involves densely packed stems, reinforce the florist's foam with small-mesh wire netting stretched over it and tucked into the rim.

Unusual Containers

Attractive boxes, such as old-fashioned mahogany and mother of pearl, papier mâché, ebony and porcupine quill, shell or printed tin, can make enchanting containers for dried flowers. If the lid is removable (or lost), there are more options than if there is a hinged lid, but even that can be turned to advantage.

Dried flowers can also be built up on a flat base. Florist's foam is impaled on florist's spikes, then fixed to the base with mastic. If necessary, glue felt to the underside of the base to prevent it scratching furniture; use the base as a template. As well as the cup-less saucers mentioned above, ceramic tiles in bright, clear colours would make attractive bases for small arrangements. Thick straw place mats; trivets; attractive pieces of polished slate, marble or granite; cross cuts of wood; and wooden bread or cheese boards are all suitable. Large pieces of driftwood can act as three-dimensional bases, with clusters of dried flowers tucked into suitable hollows, such as the space created by forking branches.

Smoking is less popular than it used to be, and many ashtrays are redundant as a result. With their wide bases and shallow rims, they are excellent for dried flowers, which can be arranged to conceal any semi-circular cigarette indentations.

There are as many variations of traditional baskets as there are patterns of fishermen's sweaters – if not more! If room allows, display empty baskets as well as full ones, or, as shown, a happy mixture of both.

In the Garden

The trend today towards low-maintenance gardens is understandable, but annuals often become innocent victims of the quest for plants that need no attention. Annuals, by their very nature, need replacing on a yearly basis, although some, such as love-in-a-mist, unfailingly self seed. Looking more positively at annuals, their short life span provides an opportunity for a variety of options. Every year you can try something different, eliminating mistakes – whether horticultural or aesthetic – and repeating successes. Because you can build up stocks of dried flowers, your choice of annuals can exactly mirror your needs: you may have masses of dried ammobium left from the previous year, for example, but want to try out gomphrena.

Half-hardy annuals require extra care; they must be started off under glass in late winter or early spring, and grown on indoors until ready for transplanting after the last frosts. Some hardy annuals also benefit from an early start under glass, especially where summers are unreliable. Gardening and flower arranging are allied interests, though, and if you enjoy one, chances are you enjoy the other, and it is a labour of love.

Choosing Hardy and Half-hardy Annuals

Young bedding plants of some annuals suitable for preserving, such as Prince of Wales's feather, are also sold in garden centres in late spring. It is a much more expensive way to obtain material, but is useful if you lack the facilities or patience for starting plants from seed.

In large gardens, areas of the kitchen garden can be given over to growing annuals for cutting, so that flower decorations for the house need not involve diminishing the beauty of the garden. It is more often, however, a question of compromise, of accommodating annuals in mixed beds and borders, and picking fewer than you possibly might, to leave a splash of colour in the garden.

Unless you have masses of space, try to grow the more unusual annuals, as helichrysum and statice are easily and inexpensively available. What else is available ready-dried obviously varies from one place to another, but if you can buy it at a reasonable price, there is little point in taking up valuable garden space growing it.

As well as the helichrysum (H. *bracteatum*) or strawflower, there are other species of everlasting daisy, or immortelles from the *Compositae* family. These are the flowers that dry virtually by themselves, with just a minimum of air drying (see pages 39-43) to finish them off. The sand flower, or winged everlasting (*Ammobium alatum*) has typical white daisy flowers with bright yellow centres. The variety 'Grandiflora' has the largest flowers, worth seeking out because the species has rather small flowers in relation to its long, flattened stems. (Wiring the flowers into small bunches before using is another alternative.)

The genus *Helipterum*, commonly called sunrays, includes two very useful species, but the nomenclature is particularly confusing. The Swan River everlasting (H. *manglesii*, sometimes called *Rhodanthe manglessi*), has papery daisies ranging from white to red in colour. *Helipterum roseum*, sometimes sold as *Acroclinium roseum*, has pink, red or white daisy-shaped flowers, up to 5cm (2in) across, with typical yellow centres. Helipterums have easily breakable slender, wiry stems; many people wire the flowers before drying.

Slender and star like, with more delicate petals, is *Xeranthemum annuum*, called immortelle in America. The single or double flowers range from purple to white, and mixed seed is usually available.

Cupid's dart (*Catananche caerulea*), has silvery pointed bracts as attractive as its purple-pink, daisy-like flowers. It is technically a perennial, but needs a warm spot to do well and is usually grown as a half-hardy annual.

Thistles are, to the non-botanist, unexpected members of the daisy family; like the more usual 'daisy' flowers, there are many useful annuals for drying. Safflower, or dyer's greenwood (*Carthamus tinctorius*) is attractive when its closed buds resemble green rosebuds, or open, when its thread-like orange centres

Frost, though exquisite in itself, will damage any naturally dried material left in the garden over winter. A hard ground frost can also put paid, at least temporarily, to any serious gardening, especially digging. Use your allotted gardening time, and the long dark evenings, to browse through seed and plant catalogues.

appear. On a larger scale is the blessed thistle (*Silybum marianum*), with deep violet tufts. Largest of all is the giant thistle (*Onopordum acanthium*), which reaches 2.4m (8ft) or more. The latter is biennial, but self seeds so prolifically that the only effort involved is the initial planting – and perhaps weeding out unwanted seedlings thereafter! Cornflower (*Centaurea cyanus*) and sweet sultan (*C. moschata*), are easy-to-grow *Compositae*; old-fashioned blue cornflowers are particularly useful, as blue is a rare colour among easily dried flowers.

The *Amaranthaceae* family, though much smaller than *Compositae*, has a great deal to offer. Love-lies-bleeding, or the velvet or tassel flower (*Amaranthus caudatus*, A. *hybridus*), is a half-hardy, tropical annual, useful for its gracefully pendulous inflorescences. There are crimson, green, yellow and white-flowered forms available. Pick when about half the small flowers are open, or the whole lot will disintegrate, then dry upright in a small amount of water. Related to amaranthus is another Victorian favourite, the cockscomb (*Celosia argentea cristata*). Its velvety convoluted inflorescences look like red, gold or pink coral, though they are also likened to brains, rather unkindly. Hang them upside down to dry. Some people leave the roots attached while drying.

Prince of Wales's feathers (*Celosia argentea plumosa*) carries fluffy, erect, pyramidal plumes in red or yellow. A third useful relative is the globe amaranth (*Gomphrena globosa*), whose round, papery clover-like flowers come in shades of purple, red, pink, white or yellow. The globe amaranth has weak stems; many people treat it like helichrysum, wiring up the stem before or part-way through drying. The drawback of *Amaranthaceae*, from the point of view of their contribution to the garden, is that the plants tend to be coarse in form and foliage, with the popular dwarf cultivars particularly unnatural looking.

Small zinnias can be dried in silica gel; large, double ones are definitely difficult. Giant African marigolds can be air dried, though they shrink substantially; their weak stems need wire through the centre before being hung up to dry. The papery bracts of clary (*Salvia horminum*), in shades of red, pink, blue or white, air dry well.

Love-in-a-mist (*Nigella damascena*) is an uncommon member of the buttercup family, Ranunculaceae, and one of best annuals for drying. The clear-blue flowers can be air dried, but they are fragile and it is the blimp-like seed pod, with the ruff of lacy leaves beneath, which are most valuable. If left to the end of the season, they dry naturally to a pale beige, but if harvested earlier and air dried they retain their green or maroon-striped hue. Another surprising relative of buttercups is delphinium, and the annual delphinium, or larkspur (*Consolida regalis*), is useful for its spikes of pink, blue or white flowers. Larkspur is sold in vast quantities fresh but also ready-dried.

Bells of Ireland (*Moluccella laevis*) is a half-hardy annual with spikes of unmistakable green, bell-shaped bracts. These can be air dried, or preserved with silica or glycerine; colours vary according to method. It is a member of the *Labiatae* family, as is clary; the plants of this family often have attractive bracts set in whorls on the flower spike.

Annual hollyhocks (*Althaea* spp and cvs) and mallows (*Lavatera* spp and cvs), like their perennial cousins, provide flat, fat seed heads, and the flowers themselves can also be air dried. The annual opium poppy (*Papaver somniferum*) has huge, blowsy blooms followed by enormous seed capsules; the flowers can be enjoyed once in the garden, then their pods – among the largest of the genus – used in dried arrangements. Opium poppy self sows from one year to the next.

The annual sunflower (*Helianthus annuus*) has huge solitary heads, which eventually form row upon row of tightly packed seeds. Sunflower heads dry easily, but are almost too big and visually overpowering to be mixed with other flowers. There are many similar but small annual rudbeckias that dry well and are better 'mixers'.

Ornamental annual grasses worth growing include hare's tail, or rabbit's tail grass (*Lagurus ovatus*), instantly identifiable for its soft, fluffy inflorescences. It needs a warm garden to do really well. Squirrel's tail grass (*Hordeum juba-*

tum) has dense, attractively arching awns. Job's tears (*Coix lacryma-jobi*) is a plant much loved by Victorians for its hanging clusters of shiny, pearly grey or black seeds. Both greater and lesser quaking grass (B*riza maxima*, B.*minor*) have trembling locket-shaped seed heads. Lastly, animated oat (A*vena sterilis*), so called because its bristle-like awns move with changes of moisture in the air.

The shoo-fly plant, or apple of Peru (N*icandra physalodes*) has papery calyces surrounding a small inedible fruit, like a Chinese lantern. Though the colour of the fresh calyx varies from green to rich blue-black, it tends to dry a pale beige. Unfortunately, like the latter, the shoo-fly plant is coarse looking, though its light-blue, bell-shaped flowers are modestly attractive.

S*tatice sinuatum* is the ordinary dried statice; more interesting and worth growing is the rat's tail statice (S. *suworowii*), with long, purple pink narrow spikes.

Seeds

You can buy seeds of wild flowers and ornamental annual grasses, either single species or mixed collections, from specialist seedsmen, and some of the major seedsmen as well. Although the main idea of growing wild flowers in a garden is one of conservancy, it can also be done for harvesting flowers and pods for drying. Teasel (D*ipsacus fullonum*), for example, can be difficult to find in the wild. You can also buy specially selected mixed seeds of flowers suitable for drying; though these may be fun to try, the plants chosen do not always have the same cultivation needs or growth rates, so success is bound to be less than total.

Seeds of ornamental kale and cabbages are readily available, usually in mixtures. Though edible, they dry extremely well, and are usually grown in the flower garden. They are biennials, but usually grown as hardy or half-hardy annuals, and their rosettes of plain, crinkled or frilly leaves come in shades of white, pink, grey, cream, red and purple, often with contrasting veins or prettily variegated.

In the vegetable garden proper, onions and leeks left to go to seed produce glorious, rounded heads, every bit as attractive as those of ornamental alliums. Carrot flowers, though not allowed to develop in conventional vegetable growing, are obvious cousins of cow parsley, and can be air dried. Annual and biennial umbellifer herbs – dill, chervil, angelica, parsley, fennel, coriander and caraway – are equally useful.

If you have the space, try ornamental gourds – otherwise, buy them ready dried. More unusual is the wild cucumber vine (E*chinocystis lobata*). A native of North America, it is cultivated elsewhere as much for its rampant growth, up to 6m (20ft) in a single season, and its attractive maple-like leaves, as for its spiny, light-weight fruits. These are green when unripe, and dry an attractive shade of tan, surrounded by curling tendrils. Treat like dried clematis, hanging the weak stems through other material.

Growing Half-hardy Annuals from Seed

The difference between hardy and half-hardy annuals is their tolerance of frost. In northern temperate climates, the amount of time between the last spring frost and first autumn one is usually insufficient for some plants – often of tropical origin – to flower and set seed. They are therefore started off indoors in warmth, then planted out when all danger of frost is over.

The dividing line between half-hardy and hardy annuals is not always clear. Seed catalogues and books sometimes seemingly contradict each other or state, 'Treat as hardy or half-hardy annual'. Some half-hardy annuals – celosias, for example and bells of Ireland – must be started off under glass. Other frost-tender plants can also be sown outdoors in late April or early May, to give a short display in late summer and early autumn. Some perfectly hardy annuals flower earlier if started under glass than if sown outdoors. By using both techniques you get a longer season of display, important if the flowers form part of the ornamental garden as well as a source of material for drying. (See pages 33, 39-43).

Do not sow plants under glass too early; late February or even March is soon enough, otherwise the seedlings will have grown too big and

Quaking grass, in both its larger and smaller forms (Briza maxima, B. minima respectively) has a charming delicacy. A hardy annual, quaking grass thrives in sunny, warm conditions and poorish soils. As a 'filler' for dried flower displays, it makes an unusual alternative to gypsophila.

Red-barked willow (Salix alba 'Chermesina') and yellow-barked willow (S.a. 'Vitellina') are invaluable for dried flower displays. They add height, bulk and colour, and can be used as the foundation for wreaths.

require planting outdoors before the weather is warm enough. Use seed trays or individual pots, if the seeds are large enough to handle. Compressed peat pots and flat, expandable peat discs are ideal, as the seedlings can be planted straight into the ground. If you are raising large quantities of plants, you might consider buying peat blocking compost, which is pressed in cube-shaped modules with a special tool. Plastic seed trays divided into individual compartments are also sensible, as the seedlings' roots do not become tangled.

Use John Innes seed compost or another peat-based equivalent, pressing the compost down lightly with your fingertips and finishing with a level surface. Leave 1cm (½in) gap between the surface of the compost and the rim of the tray or pot, to allow for watering. Water lightly before sowing; the compost should be damp but not saturated. Partially submerge the tray or pot in a basin of water, so the moisture is absorbed from underneath; remove the container when the surface darkens. Alternatively, use a spray gun, or a watering can fitted with a fine rose. Soak peat discs until they are fully expanded.

If the seeds are tiny, sow thinly; mixing them with a small quantity of silver sand gives a more even distribution. Sow seeds large enough to handle 2.5cm (1in) apart each way. A certain number of seeds inevitably fail to germinate, so if you are sowing seeds individually, sow a few extra; you can also sow two seeds per pot, and remove the weaker one.

After sowing, cover the seeds to their own depth with sifted compost; do not cover fine seeds. If you are using a propagator, replace the lid, otherwise cover the trays or pots with black plastic or a pane of glass, then a sheet of brown paper. Temperature needs vary, but 13-16°C (55-60°F) is a good guide; follow directions on the seed packet. No additional watering should be necessary; if any droplets condense on the glass or propagator lid, wipe them off.

Germination times also vary, but germination usually takes place within a month. Once the seedlings appear, gradually expose them to more light, and increase the air circulation to prevent damping off. If they are grown on a window sill, turn the pots or trays round daily, to prevent the seedlings growing in one direction, towards the source of light.

When the seedlings are large enough to handle, usually when two seed leaves and one or two true leaves have appeared, prick them out. If left longer, the seedlings are liable to become spindly and drawn out, and the shock of transplanting also increases. Using the pointed end of a plastic plant label, lever each seedling out, being careful not to damage the roots. Use a low-nutrient compost, such as John Innes no 1 or 2. Space them 5cm (2in) apart in each direction, making the holes in the compost with a dibber or pencil. The hole should be deep and wide enough to comfortably take the roots and most of the stem. Water lightly and provide shade for a day or two.

Useful Garden Prunings

Although garden prunings usually end up on the bonfire, some are excellent raw material for dried flower displays. Well chosen branches can add bulk and structure to a traditional dried flower arrangement, and can also create a sculptural, contemporary effect. Branches of some deciduous and evergreen shrubs and trees can be preserved with their foliage intact, to provide mass, colour and interest to all sorts of arrangements (see pages 135-137).

While pruning at the wrong time of year is rarely fatal to a plant, it can be self defeating, in that you may be cutting off the wood that carries the following season's flowers. Most deciduous shrubs, especially those that flower on new wood, are best pruned when dormant, from late autumn until spring. These prunings are usually harder and less flexible than prunings taken in spring or early summer. (Deciduous shrubs, trees and climbers that flower on the previous year's wood are usually pruned then, immediately after flowering.) Most evergreens are pruned in mid-spring, once they start into growth, but with most of the growing season left for recovery. Try to strike a reasonable balance between your plants' horticultural needs, and your own needs for flower arrangements.

Unless pruning back to ground level, always cut just above a node, to minimize die back and encourage side shoots to break. Removing overcrowded or crossing branches improves the appearance of the shrub as well as providing raw material for arranging. Lastly, you have to live with what you leave behind, and a slow-growing shrub may take years to recover from impulsive pruning, to benefit a single evening's dinner party.

In the case of hedge pruning, however, you can combine pruning and harvesting in one operation. Box hedges are kept formal by regular clipping; the little sprigs that are normally swept up are ideal for glycerining. They turn a pleasing pale beige, and can form the basis of numerous miniature arrangements. In seaside gardens, hedges are sometimes planted of *Griselinia littoralis* or escallonia, both of which take well to glycerining; and the winter pruning of thorn hedges provides an infinite supply of interestingly shaped twigs.

Branches can provide colour as well as bulk and form. Red-bark dogwood (*Cornus alba* 'Sibirica'), yellow-bark dogwood (*C. stolonifera* 'Flaviramea'), scarlet willow (*Salix alba* 'Chermesina') and golden willow (*S.a.* 'Vitellina') have the most pronounced colour on young growth. This is also true of violet-bark willow, *S. daphnoides*; violet-barked box elder (*Acer negundo violaceum*); and *Rubus cockburnianus*, the waxy white arching branches of which are strikingly elegant. Annual or biennial pruning encourages a continuous supply of intensely coloured new wood, providing marvellous raw material for dried flower displays at the same time. (The coral-bark maple, *Acer palmatum* 'Senkaki' has beautiful red young wood, but it is slow growing and should be pruned with the greatest restraint to avoid spoiling the plant.)

Jew's mallow (*Kerria japonica*) produces an abundance of slender, flexible, bright-green stems; it is a dense, suckering shrub, and the more you cut, the more suckers it produces. Japanese bitter orange (*Poncirus trifoliata*) has rigidly angular, smooth and fiercely spiny bright-green wood, but is rather slow growing, especially to start with, and is best handled with gloves and pruned with restraint.

The curiously beautiful corkscrew-like stems of contorted willow, or curly willow (*Salix matsudana* 'Tortuosa'), can be found in flower arrangements in fashionable restaurants, salons and charity galas everywhere. Stripped of its bark and ghostly pale, or sprayed with colour, curly willow is almost a cliché, but is worth using in spite of its 'yuppie' connotations. (Curly willow is extremely quick growing and makes a good-sized tree, tolerant of heavy pruning; single stems stuck in the ground in autumn or spring will take root.)

Slower growing and more tightly twisted – rather like the wool of a newly unpicked jumper – is contorted hazel, or Harry Lauder's walking stick (*Corylus avellana* 'Contorta'). It was originally found growing wild in an English hedgerow in Victorian times, and has since been propagated vegetatively. In dried flower displays, both contorted hazel and willow have a graphic effect as much as a sculptural one, as if an unseen hand has scribbled, three dimensionally, in space.

Rarer, and much prized by flower arrangers for its oriental overtones, is the willow *Salix sachalinensis* 'Sekka', sometimes sold as S. 'Setsuka'. This vigorous, wide-spreading large shrub or small tree is a male clone that produces strangely flattened and curved branches among the ordinary ones; annual hard pruning encourages the production of a higher proportion of these fasciated stems and branches. Interestingly, the common garden forsythia, F. × *intermedia* 'Spectabilis' often produces fasciated branches, and these are worth looking out for.

Some trees and shrubs have attractively angular, wing-like growths on the branches. *Euonymus alatus*, an oriental relative of the wild European spindle tree (*E. europaeus*) and the American strawberry tree (*E. americanus*) has pronounced 'wings', as do the corky branches of the American sweet gum (*Liquidamber styraciflua*), and the young branches of field maple (*Acer campestre*). (English elm branchlets have corky wings, but Dutch elm disease has decimated this source of material.)

In the fruit garden, the nobbly, spurred branches of apple, cherry, pear or plum have an

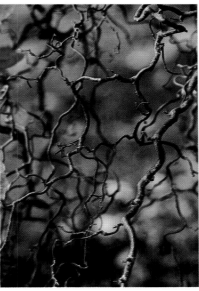

The corkscrew, contorted or curly willow (Salix matsudana 'Tortuosa') provides prunings extremely useful for modern or oriental flower displays. Like most willows it is quick growing, and generous amounts can be taken.

inbuilt character, especially if lichen covered. Branches pruned to keep the framework open, and the tree healthy and cropping well, can be used to bulk out a dried flower display, or add a single vertical accent. Even the prunings from old currant bushes can have a pleasingly sculptural quality. Mulberry branches are picturesque, but as the trees are slow growing and bleed profusely when cut, pruning is not normally done. The branches of weeping mulberry (*Morus alba* 'Pendula') are a particular treasure.

Most trees with attractively textured bark, such as eucalyptus, plane, ornamental cherries, birches and snake-bark maples, produce such bark only on older trunks and primary branches, but dead tree trunks may be sawn crossways to form rustic bases for arrangements and the branches used as the framework for dramatic, large-scale dried flower trees.

pine cone

ficus seed pod

contorted willow

cork oak bark

oak galls

Although not usually thought of as a woody shrub, heather is a good filler in dried arrangements, and should be pruned after flowering in any case, to keep it compact. Cultivars with strikingly coloured foliage are worth using for colour alone, but judiciously clip a few flowering sprigs for drying as well. (See pages 39-43).

Pussy willow is a popular spring feature, with the catkin-covered branches as useful in dried arrangements as fresh ones. *Salix melanostachys,* also known as S. 'Kueneko'; S. 'Kurome', and S. 'Kuroyanagi', has handsome black catkins with bright-red anthers, which gradually change to yellow. Ordinary grey pussy willow catkins have an endearing charm, and are more easily available. Weeping willow, pussy willow and broom are useful for fashioning into tightly curved semi-circles, for abstract arrangements. Soak the branches for a few hours, then tie them to a lamp shade ring or kitchen ring mould and leave to dry.

Though not entirely hardy, *Edgeworthia papyrifera* is worth growing for the remarkably elegant and supple branches. They are much used in oriental flower arrangements. The plant's Japanese name, mitsumata, means three-branched, and refers to its tendency to subdivide into three branches, rather than the more usual two. Mitsumata is sometimes available, bleached and dried, from oriental stores, and can be steamed and then shaped.

Broad-leafed evergreen prunings worth preserving include elaeagnus, mahonia, eucalyptus, box, evergreen magnolia and laurel. Beech and, less commonly, birch, are the two deciduous trees commonly preserved with foliage intact. (see pages 135-137.)

Of the climbers, the gracefully twisting, pale, woody old growth of wisteria, clematis, honeysuckle, and ornamental and edible grape vine can be used as instant sculpture, while the more flexible, young growth makes an excellent base for wreaths, garlands and swags. (Grape vines are traditionally pruned in late autumn or early winter, to minimize the loss of sap.)

sweet chestnut

heather

oak

hazel

beech

larch

plane

willow

67

In the Wild

The division of woody material into garden and wild plants is an uneasy one, because all garden species and many cultivars occur or once occurred somewhere in the wild: one gardener's treasure is proverbially another gardener's weed. Many cultivars of garden origin have counterparts in the wild with basically similar qualities. Ivy (Hedera spp) for example, is among the humblest of woodland plants and yet also the subject of commercial breeding, with a whole range of variegated or otherwise sophisticated cultivars available in garden centres. There are dozens of wild willows, as charming in appearance as the many dozens of sophisticated garden cultivars. Then, too, large gardens may well contain forest trees or a genuinely wild garden within its boundaries. Nonetheless, woodland walks are a pleasant pastime, and there are treasures to be found.

Collecting from the wild is a state of mind as well as a physical activity. On the positive side, it is an exercise in discovering the wealth of raw material, available for free, all around you. On the other hand, it is human nature to take raw material in more generous quantities from 'anonymous' territory than from one's own garden. Doing so in a way that harms the source – ripping or breaking branches rather than cleanly cutting them, or pulling up plants by the roots, for example – is irresponsible and, in the long term, counter-productive. (It may also be illegal – see page 70.) Try to treat the plants as if they were yours. Do not take more than you need, although taking two or three branches from one type of tree or shrub gives you more flexibility than a single branch, and makes it easier to build up a coherent display.

Branches and Twigs

Of the trees in temperate climate woodlands, the Betulaceae family, which includes hazel, alder and birch, offers a great deal to flower arrangers. All carry charming catkins in season, but are equally attractive in their skeletal, bare form. (They are well represented in gardens by cut-leafed, yellow- or purple-leafed, ornamental-barked and weeping cultivars; and forms with brightly coloured catkins.)

The slender, slightly horizontal and much-branched stems of hazel are excellent 'bones' for a modern display, and as the basis of dried flower trees. Hazel is airy in feeling, and one or two branches can command a great deal of space. Because hazel is low-growing, wide-spreading and suckering, good material is usually within easy reach.

Alder branches are heavier looking and more intricate than hazel (black dye was traditionally made from alder bark). Alder is at its most charming when hung with its clusters of slender male catkins and long-lasting, lantern-like female fruits. The latter are formed in summer and last until the following spring, gradually turning from green to black. Such 'pre-decorated' branches can form the bulk of a display, with perhaps a single cluster of dried flowers used as a focal point. When not in fruit, the branches can themselves be hung with dried flowers. Alder is a tree of stream-side, bog and waterlogged ground, and can be as difficult to get to as hazel is easy.

Birch has graceful, elegant and flexible bare branches, and can also be preserved in leaf with glycerine (see page 135). Birch twigs can be used to decorate the handle, rim or base of a basket, stitched in place with raffia or string. Used vertically, tightly tied bunches of birch twigs can form the trunk of a dried-flower tree, or form the outer skin of an unusual container (see page 109.) The catkin-laden branchlets are excellent for breaking up the outline of tight, heavy floral displays, and add in delicacy what they lack in colour. (Besom brooms are tradi-tionally made of birch, and can be taken apart as a source of twigs in a floral 'emergency'.)

Dormant larch, with its soft needles shed but its clusters of cones attached, is always worth collecting. The flexible, arching larch branches can evoke a starkly modern feel or an old-fashioned, country cottage one, depending on how and with what it is used.

The aerial roots of ivy, and its non-climbing fertile branches, are shiny white when peeled and beautifully sculptural. Large sections of

A frosted hogweed, left, in deepest winter. Frost can transform the humblest of weeds into wonderful miniature sculptures.

Ivy's modest green flowers are followed by green berries which ripen to black by the time Christmas arrives. Though there are countless named garden forms, the wild species (Hedera helix), above, is equally beautiful, and is vigorous enough to be frequently cut.

dead ivy root may have already been stripped and bleached by the sun, and can be easily prised from a tree trunk or wall, and cut into smaller pieces.

Wilderness implies the presence of plants in all stages of life and death, whereas a garden is usually kept tidily healthy and spotless. Debris such as sun-bleached roots and branches, and chunks of hollow trunk or tree stump, such as yew, are useful raw material to retrieve from a woodland floor. So, too, are large sections of bark, such as birch, which can serve as the base for a display. Even blackened and spineless branches of burnt gorse have their aesthetic uses; these and heather can be found on moorland and heath terrain. Rotten wood, however, is not worth the effort of carrying home, although basically sound hard wood with small areas of rot can be saved.

Very exposed, windy sites, such as the seaside or mountainous regions, often have trees and shrubs which are dwarfed or twisted by their harsh environments. The one-sided, horizontal growth on trees that results from a strongly directional wind is excellent for modern dried flower display. Sea buckthorn (Hippophae rhamnoides) with its angular, spine-tipped twigs, and American manzanita, with its twisted, angular, thorny branches, are always worth collecting. Thorny wood, such as blackthorn and hawthorn, is generally 'characterful', useful for dramatic, rather than soft or feminine, displays.

Conservation

Older books on flower arranging occasionally suggest collecting nests from the wild, to enhance a dried flower 'tree' or as a container for dried flowers. Today, conservation is of primary concern and taking a bird's nest, or being in possession of a bird's nest (except in one's garden) is against the law. On a more pragmatic level, newly abandoned birds' nests are sometimes filthy with droppings, as parent birds tend to become less tidy as the baby birds grow older. It is easy to create a nest of sphagnum or bun moss, twigs, straw and dried grasses, fixed round a shallow bowl or cocotte which can then be lined with more of the same.

It is perfectly acceptable to collect oak branches with ball-like oak apple galls, and the similar marble galls, both made by wasps. (By mid-autumn, the larvae which originally made their home in the galls will have emerged through small holes and gone elsewhere.) Spraying oak-gall branches silver or gold for Christmas will camouflage the origins of the 'Christmas balls' from all but the keenest natural historian.

Another pun on nature is to glue oak galls to the more graceful branches of dormant or dead beech. This is now done commercially by up-market florists, much to the amusement of botanists.

Preparing Dead Branches and Roots

Most branches are clean enough to use as they are, and any chosen for their lichen should have as little as possible done to them, to preserve the lichen intact. (Touching the lichen, particularly once dry, can dislodge it, so handle as little as possible.) Wood bleached silvery grey by the sun should also be handled with great care, as the colour is only on the surface, and can be damaged by scrubbing.

Material picked up from the ground, 'soiled' in the literal or figurative sense, should be washed thoroughly, using water, detergent and a wire brush. Remove any rotten bits beforehand, using a small chisel, knife or screwdriver. If you are worried about bringing creatures indoors, shake the wood to give woodlice et al a fair chance to escape, then soak the wood in diluted disinfectant, making sure that all parts are submerged. Dry the wood outdoors in the sun, in an airing cupboard, or anywhere else warm.

To remove the bark of freshly picked willow, ivy, wisteria or other wood, soak it in water for several days, then scrape it off.

To bleach wood, which also puts paid to creatures, submerge it overnight in a 50/50 mixture of bleach and water. Bleach tends to yellow the wood as it lightens its natural colour. You can also bleach the wood by dissolving 15g (1 tbls) oxalic acid crystals in 1L (34 fl oz) water, then soaking the wood, completely submerged, for ten minutes and washing it immediately with warm water. Dry as above.

Techniques – Wiring

Once you have the knack, you can wire flowers quickly and almost without thinking, in the way that skilled knitters can talk or watch television as they work on intricate patterns. The most skilled wiring is discreet and allows the natural beauty of flowers, seed pods or foliage to take precedence.

As well as providing stems for flowers whose own stems are weak, brittle or ungainly thick when dried, wiring also minimizes waste, as broken-stemmed or stemless flower heads can be put to good use. It also allows you to achieve dense masses of colour. And although the technique is associated with formal displays, wiring can be an unseen aid to casual, informal arrangements.

Florists sell wired helichrysums, but it is more economical to wire your own. When the flowers are fresh, wire can be easily inserted into the head; but staining sometimes occurs. (The flower and stem contract as they dry, tightening around the wire.) Although it is difficult to push the wire in to a dried head, there is less risk of stain. Best is to partially dry flowers for a few days, insert the wires, then re-hang to finish drying.

Wiring Flowers

To wire fresh or semi-dried helichrysums, cut the stems, leaving a 13 mm (½in) stub, then push a medium-gauge wire (see page 152), 15-20cm (6-8in) long, through the centre of the stub from underneath, until 5cm (2in) of wire comes through the top of the flower. Bend the top of the wire over to form a 6mm (¼in) hook, then carefully retract the wire, pulling from underneath, until the hook firmly engages in the flower. Cover the wire with florist's tape, starting under the flower head. Stretch the tape at right angles to the wire, go round it a couple of times, then proceed taping diagonally down the wire, twisting the wire around, not the tape, and overlapping the tape slightly. Cut the tape.

Wiring helichrysums

Cut the helichrysum stem, leaving a short stub, about 13 mm (½ in) long. Using a medium-gauge stub wire, 15-20 cm (6-8 in) long, push it through the centre of the flower head, from the underneath upwards. Stop when 5 cm (2 in) of wire comes through the top of the flower.

Form a small hook at the top of the wire, then carefully pull downwards from the bottom, until the hook engages in the centre of the flower.

Cover the wire with florist's tape, working diagonally from the flower heads downwards. As you proceed, twist the wire, not the tape. To finish, cut the tape and pinch it to the wire.

71

Wiring florist's roses

Cut the stem 2.5 cm (1 in) below the flower head.

Place the medium-gauge stub wire alongside the remaining stem. Using reel wire, bind the two together. Work upwards to the underside of the flower, then back down along the stem, well beyond the overlap.

Finish with florist's tape, working the tape diagonally down the wire, and overlapping it slightly as you proceed.

Florist's roses can be air dried on their own stems, although the flowers may eventually droop at the neck, when displayed right-way up. Although it is not absolutely necessary, some people, as a precaution, wire up the heads. To do this, cut the stem 2.5cm (1in) below the flower, then place a medium-gauge stub wire next to the remaining stem. Bind with reel wire, running a short length of it along the overlap up to the underside of the flower, then coming back down the stem, twisting tightly as you proceed, well beyond the overlap. Finish with florist's tape. Fully dried helichrysums, with stems too brittle to insert a stub wire can also be treated in this way.

Shorten the stems of fresh flowers to be dried in desiccant (see page 132), so the flowers can be totally covered with desiccant, and the lid of the container shuts properly. Cut to 2.5cm (1in), and push in short stub wires, gauged according to the weight of the desiccated flower, and making sure they do not project through the top of the flower. Treat woody stems as for roses above, using reel wire to bind the stub wire next to the stem. Once preserved, place a wire of the desired length alongside the original short wire and touching the underside of the flower. Wire both together, using reel wire, and cover with florist's tape.

To add length to a sturdy natural stem of dried material, bend a medium gauge stub wire, about twice as long as the intended length, in half. Place the stem in the bend, with one wire running alongside it. Twist the other wire back over it as tightly as possible, and continue twisting diagonally along until finished, pinching tightly as you twist. If the join will be visible in the display, tape over both the natural stem and extension.

This same method of extension also works with tight bunches of a single type of flower. This is especially useful if you want intense colour from naturally small or airy flowers, such as larkspur, ammobium or gypsophila; or if you are building up a dense display and lack space for insertion in the dried florist's foam or wire netting. Place up to a dozen stems, depending on their weight and thickness, of roughly the same length, in a bunch, then wire the bunch, using reel wire, to a single wire. The shorter the natural stems, the more compact you can make the material. Delicate grasses sometimes benefit from bunching in this manner, and are easier to handle.

Cones

Pine and other conifer cones need false stems, as they have none of their own. One method is to bend a single stub wire around a row of scales near the base of a cone, with one side roughly twice as long as the other. Pull the wire tightly so it slots into a row of scales, then bend the two ends down, twisting the wires together, to form a stem. For large, heavy cones, use two parallel wires, one on each side of the cone, again towards the base. Twist the wires together, at the sides of the cone, then bend them down towards the base and twist both sets together. Tape with brown tape, if the stems are going to be visible in the finished display.

Nuts

Walnuts, Brazil nuts, hazel nuts, and so on, are wonderful raw material for Christmas decorations, but they do need wiring before they can be used. Although sweet and horse chestnuts, with their attractive casings, can be displayed on the branch, they are also excellent used individually, in which case they need wiring up as well. Many nuts and nut casings have a narrow join where two halves meet, and this is usually softer than the surrounding shells. With a drill or red-hot wire or skewer, make a hole in the top centre of the join, then insert a wire or tiny metal eye on a screw, for use with thread or ribbon. Fresh walnuts and conkers can be pierced directly with heavy-gauge wire; push the wire deeply into the nut, until it is thoroughly imbedded. Or run a lightweight wire along this shallow channel, twisting the ends of the wire firmly at the bottom, to form 'stems'; the wire in the join is inconspicuous.

Branches

Branches, whether leafless or with preserved leaves, can be extended as above. If very heavy, use bamboo canes or dowels for sup-

Wiring cones and nuts

Bend a medium-gauge stub wire around a row of scales near the base of the cone, with one side of the wire roughly twice as long as the other.

Pull the wire tightly so that it slots into the scales, then bend the two ends down, twisting the wires together to join them.

Use a heated skewer, wire or small screwdriver to pierce a hole through tough shells. Insert a stub wire, or tiny metal eye on a screw, for use with thread or ribbon.

Adding gold-sprayed cones and ribbon bows will transform a swag of artificial fir tree foliage into a very attractive Christmas decoration.

port. Wire up single leaves, such as *Fatsia japonica* after they are preserved. Using silver reel wire, make a single small stitch across the midrib on the upper surface, a third of the way up the leaf. Bring the two wire ends through to the underside of the leaf, then run them down the centre of the leaf, towards the stalk. Twist one wire around the leaf stalk, the other wire, and a stub wire, then tape. Sellotaping a stub wire to the underside of the leaf, along the midrib, works with some leaves. Leaves with long stalks can be attached directly to a stub wire by binding stalk and stub wire together with reel wire, then taping both.

A taped wire does not look natural, but it looks better than shiny, exposed wire and does remain flexible. An alternative to tape is to use a hollow or pithy stem of another plant, to conceal the wire. Grasses, such as wild oats, and garden flowers, such as delphinium, dahlia, love-lies-bleeding, *Iris sibirica*, columbine, goldenrod, achillea and opium poppy have suitable stems. Save these stems whenever you remove the flowers for wiring up separately; some people grow a few extra solely for the stems. The one drawback of this natural form of concealment is that the stems can be inflexible.

It is also possible to bypass using wires for lightweight flower heads, and use strong natural stems to replace weaker ones. If there is a stub remaining on the flower head, insert it, with a dab of quick-drying glue, into the top of the replacement stem; the closer the fit, the less risk of later breakage. Otherwise, make a tiny hole, using a thick wire, in the centre of the flower to be mounted. Insert the bottom end of the replacement stem, with a bit of its flower or seed head left on to act as a plug, into the top of the flower. Gently pull the replacement stem down through the hole in the flower head, until the flower or seed head locks into position.

Wreaths and Swags

Since the Renaissance, wreaths have been a symbol of Christianity, and a Christmas wreath or swag is the *sine qua non* of many people's festive decorations. Swags of Indian corn have decorated countless Thanksgiving celebrations and harvest festivals. Dried flower wreaths or swags can also convey the essence of spring or summer, with a freshness and novelty sometimes lacking in conventional Christmas or harvest decorations.

Swags and wreaths should be generously full; any sight of florist's foam or wire mesh netting counteracts all feelings of bounty. Building up depth, so that the flowers, foliage, seed pods and cones create a sculptured surface and variation in outline, is generally more attractive than using them with uniformly short stems, so that they hug the foundation like wallpaper. A focal point, such as a bow or cluster of large-scale dried material, adds interest, but all-over textures can be equally attractive.

Though wreaths and swags traditionally decorate front doors, most dried material (except for cones) is unsuitable for outdoor use. An overhanging roof or porch gives some protection against direct rain and snow, but they often blow sideways, and atmospheric moisture is just as destructive. Internal walls and doors are better positions, although a few hours outdoors on Christmas Day, given fine weather, does no harm.

Bases Florist's foam bases, in round and oval shapes and various sizes, have made making dried flower wreaths a foolproof exercise, and a well-covered wreath gives no indication of its manufactured foundation. On the other hand, old-fashioned alternatives – wire mesh netting, or rings of dried branches, vine stems or Chinese gooseberry stems (see page 59) can make good bases, as their slight asymmetry and imperfections are charming. Cut equal lengths of branch or stem, about 1m (3ft) long. Form the first one into a circle, then secure the two ends together with reel wire. Twine the remaining lengths of branch or stem, one at a time, around this framework, then leave to dry.

Florists occasionally use old-fashioned wire wreath frames, around which moss is packed, then held in place with twine or reel wire wrapped round it and the frame. The most basic wreaths can be built up on lampshade rings, or wire coat hangers bent into a circle, then covered with moss wrapped with reel wire. Plaited or twisted and tied raffia can also be used as a covering.

Swags are similar to wreaths in that they are wall hung decorations, but instead of an open centre, they tend to be solid, and roughly triangular, oval or rectangular in shape. Some swags are simply short lengths of garlands, hung vertically (see pages 110-111). Swags are often used in pairs, one on either side of a window or mirror. Hanging several swags of similar or complementary design on a blank wall is an inexpensive way to create a bold effect. Swags can be built on foundations of florist's foam or moss, covered with wire mesh netting for extra strength; or consist of an upside-down bouquet of dried material, facing in one direction, rather than designed to be seen in the round.

Peg-board, cut to a suitable shape, can also be used as a foundation, with the dried material wired through the holes. Traditional swags have no backing visible, but they are sometimes attached to large, flat, decorative bases, such as cork, wood or velvet-covered board, to make wall plaques. For grand occasions or settings, multiple swags can be made by fixing two or three foundations onto a long length of dowel, leaving space between each.

Work on a wreath or swag in a vertical position to get the proper effect; one which seems balanced and well covered from above may appear patchy seen vertically. The exceptions are bouquet-type swags, which have to be built up on a flat surface, and wreaths meant to be seen horizontally – those displayed as the centre-piece of a dining-table, for example, or, jovially, round the neck of a statue or bust. To hang, either hook the wreath over a nail or coat hook, or fix a loop of strong twine or wire round the top, then twist it in the back to form a concealed loop. For swags, thread a wire a third of the way down from the top, in the centre of the back of a swag, and form the wire into a loop.

There are several methods of building up the material on a wreath. You can work symmetrically outwards from a single point at the top or bottom, or overlap in one direction, clockwise or anti-clockwise. The wreath can be divided visually in half, horizontally, then worked downwards in both directions from the top and

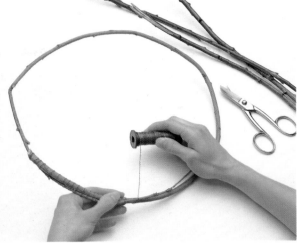

Making wreaths from branches

Using fresh, supple wood, such as willow, start the base with a single branch. Overlap the two ends and, using reel wire, bind them together to form a circle.

Begin interweaving more branches, using wire only when necessary to fix a stubborn branch in position. Tuck the ends of the branches into existing gaps, and continue until the desired thickness is reached.

Wire on decorations, such as cones and nuts. More flexible material, such as feathers, and flowers on natural stems, can simply be inserted into the tightly woven branches. Check that they are secure by giving a gentle tug; if not, reposition. The finished wreath is shown on page 82.

upwards in both directions from the bottom, to meet in the middle. These methods are particularly suitable for formal arrangements, in which flowers, cones or pods are spaced at regular intervals. You can also adapt a more artist-like approach, building up material evenly over the whole surface. Whatever method you use, check as you proceed that the material on the wreath is well balanced in order to achieve the right effect.

For a swag that is simply a front-facing bouquet, choose relatively flat material, such as grasses, bulrushes, artemisia or glycerined beech branches for the lowest layers. The uppermost layers can consist of more three-dimensional material, such as teasels or echinops, or ears of maize. Keep in mind, however, where the swag is to be displayed; material that projects too much is inconvenient and vulnerable. Start with the longest material first, to define the length. Build upwards from the lowest layer, establishing the width early on, if the longest material is not also the widest. Once the broad extremities are defined, gradually work towards the centre. Delicate material, such as gypsophila, nipplewort or dried grasses, used as edging, can give an airy lightness to an otherwise heavy-looking swag. Line up all the stems, then bind them together with wire or raffia; a ribbon bow can be used to conceal the wire.

Wreaths and swags based on cones, nuts and pods last for years. Solid designs often have a richness of texture similar to the wooden carvings of Grinling Gibbons; more skeletal wreaths of cones, nuts and pods can be decorated with fresh sprigs of conifer or long-lasting broad-leaved evergreen foliage every year. The material can be used randomly or arranged according to size, with the largest ones clustered at the top of the wreath or swag, or along the centre line, working outwards and using the smallest ones at the bottom or extremities.

Unusual wreaths can be made of branches of monkey puzzle (*Araucaria araucana*), curved into a circle and held with wire. A pair of elegant fronds of fresh sago, or fern, palm (*Cycas revoluta*), can be shaped into a starkly modern wreath. Hold each frond upside down, then twist reel wire round the stalk and continue spiralling downwards towards the tip, passing the wire between leaflets. Shape the fronds into semi-circles, then join, top and bottom, with more wire, and leave to dry.

A dried-herb wreath or swag makes a lovely culinary present, to be hung in the kitchen and used. Use sprigs of dried bay, tarragon, thyme and sage leaves, perhaps with shallots or garlic heads as 'flowers'. Sticks of cinnamon, tied into little bunches with narrow ribbons, vanilla pods and nutmeg could form the main ingredients of a 'sweet' wreath, nestling on a bed of moss studded with cloves. Simplest of all is using ready-made ropes of garlic tied to a circular wire frame.

Decorating Presents

Although there are birthdays, anniversaries and other traditional times for gift giving throughout the year, the Christmas season is the high point. Lists are drawn up and almost inevitably added to as the important date approaches. The spirit of the season becomes infectious – perhaps even manic – and second or third gifts are bought for those whose original present, on reflection, begins to seem insufficient. There are last-minute stocking fillers and wildly extravagant gestures, most of which need wrapping.

Wrapping presents should be enjoyable, and reflect the spirit in which they are given. Decorating them with dried flowers helps add a personal touch, and is surprisingly economical, as you can use up all the bits and bobs of flower heads left over from larger arrangements and other projects. You can do much of the work in advance, making up clusters and tiny bouquets, and attach them at the last minute. You can also spray dried material with gold, silver or bronze metallic paint – very handy for faded flowers and seed pods, which retain perfect form but look rather depressing and forlorn seen against the strident reds and greens of the Christmas season.

Plainly coloured wrapping paper is always a safe background, as any dried flower decorations inevitably stand out in contrast. On the other hand, high-gloss wrapping paper in a

Personalized gift wrappings can convey as much warmth and affection as the present they contain. Though time is in short supply, the closer to Christmas one gets, a quiet afternoon or evening with a box of dried flower heads, a tin or two of spray paint, and ribbons can yield dozens of lovely decorations.

single colour shows even the slightest crease or wrinkle. Patterned wrapping paper, like textured or patterned carpets, tends to hide small mistakes, and can suggest the colour scheme of the dried flower decoration. Some designs, however, are powerful and do not need further embellishment: a delicate dried-flower decoration would get lost against such a background. If in doubt, hold a small bunch against the paper, before proceeding.

Small Gifts Easier than wrapping parcels is using a self-wrapped box – one to which decorative paper or finish has been laminated by the manufacturer. These boxes come in a range of sizes, shapes and colours, and although they are relatively expensive, do eliminate all trauma and have a professionally perfect appearance. As well as boxes, there are bags, in high gloss toughened paper, with decorative ribbon handles. A small posy of dried flowers could be attached to the handle, tied with a ribbon with trailing streamers.

Some dried flowers and seed heads form an instant decoration in themselves – gold- or silver-sprayed carline thistles, allium seed heads, wild cucumbers, teasels or dried hydrangea flower heads. Bells of Ireland, sprayed gold, silver or red, become charming Christmas bells, and a cluster can be wired to the centre of a bow. A small cluster of red, ball-like craspedia looks like furry Christmas tree balls. Echinops seed heads have a similar shape, and a more subtle, silvery-blue colour, ideal against plain gold or silver paper.

One or two smallish pine cones, or a cluster of gold or silver-sprayed alder twigs, can be wired into the centre of a bow. Try a cluster of metallic-sprayed love-in-a-mist or scabious seed pods, surrounded by a haze of dried white gypsophila. For a child's present, spray a large pine cone gold, silver or even glossy dark green, wire it vertically to form a mini-Christmas tree, then decorate with tiny balls and garlands of dried florets, or even single heads of red-dyed glixia.

Cylindrical presents, such as pre-packaged bottles of drink or perfume, can be decorated with tiny garlands of flowers, or of cones and seed pods for a more masculine effect.

For Mother's Day, or birthday presents, decorate the present with tiny sachets of lavender or gauze-filled potpourris. Tied to the end of narrow satin ribbons, these can be hung in a clothes cupboard or placed in a drawer. Alternatively, a sheaf of lavender flowers, dried on the stalk and bound with a narrow ribbon, looks most attractive, although some of the tiny florets are liable to snap off. For those, of either sex, who enjoy cooking, a sheaf of cinnamon sticks tied with a bright ribbon, vanilla bean pods or sprigs of dried rosemary and bay, would make a useful and decorative finishing touch to a present. Branches of colourful dried chillis are also attractive, but need careful handling by both you and the recipient, as the peppers can cause skin rashes, which counteracts the spirit of gift giving!

It is often easier to construct the decoration than to attach it to the present. Self-wrapped boxes come into their own then, as you can make a tiny hole in the lid where you want to place the decoration, then fix it with fine wire pushed through the hole and taped to the inside of the cover. Make sure the end of the wire is well covered, to avoid damaging the present or causing scratches.

Large Gifts For larger presents, you could build up swags, wreaths or sprays of dried flowers on florist's foam, as for an ordinary table or wall decoration. Wire the florist's foam through the lid in two equidistant places, before starting. Loop each wire over the florist's foam, pushing it through two holes in the lid and twisting it together underneath the lid. (If you have the pleasure of seeing the present being opened, you can help preserve the decoration intact!)

Tiny, stemless *Compositae* flowers can be fixed, with a spot of quick-drying glue to the trailing ends of ribbon bows. You could also glue them directly onto the paper, perhaps spelling out the name in the case of a child's present, although the flowers would not be re-usable. Or make broad stripes of quick drying glue and sprinkle potpourri over, re-sprinkling until it forms a dense cover . . . extravagant, but lovely, and if the box is self wrapped, it can be re-used. Presents decorated with dried flowers need careful handling, and do not stack well. If you plan to do large-scale decoration of Christmas presents, make sure you have ample space for storage, to avoid accidental breakage.

Making Pomanders

Pomanders, or clove oranges, are one of the few presents children can make which do not look childish when finished. Pomanders, originally used to ward off disease and unpleasant household odours, were made of ambergris or herbs and spices, carried in small perforated containers of precious metal, ivory, wood or crystal. Some were moulded out of perfumed gum into solid beads, strung into bracelets and necklaces. Others still were citrus fruit stuck with cloves and dried, the form which is popular today, not only to scent cupboards, but to deter moths.

Use fresh oranges, lemons or limes; and roughly 25g (1oz) cloves for a medium-sized orange. Stud the fruit all over, leaving space between cloves to allow for shrinkage. Cloves are very hard and wearing a thimble makes the work easier. You can leave vertical gaps for ribbons, as if quartering the fruit; or insert an upholstery staple at the top, through which a ribbon can be threaded for hanging. Limes (and elderly lemons) can be very tough skinned, and you may need to prick the skin with a pin before inserting each clove. When the fruit is completely covered, roll it in your hand, gently pressing inwards, to make sure that all the cloves are pushed well in.

Wrap the fruit in tissue paper and store in a dark, dry place at room temperature for about three weeks, by which time it will dry completely. To extend its life and increase its fragrance, mix 60g (2tbls) orris-root powder with 15g (1tsp) cinnamon or cinnamon and nutmeg in a bowl. Add the citrus fruit and work the powder well into the surface, until it is coated, then store. You can also dip the cloves into oil of rosemary, lavender or geranium before insertion, but allow more time for drying.

You can add a nice touch by fixing a small posy of dried flowers to the top of the pomander, where the ribbon is attached. Or decorate the pomander, once dried, with rows of tiny flower and seed heads, such as glixia, nipple-

Making pomanders

Choose fresh citrus fruit and allow roughly 25g (1oz) cloves for a medium-sized orange. Mark out a narrow gap along the diameter for a ribbon, if wished, and begin studding the fruit with cloves. Leave space between the cloves to allow for shrinkage. Wrap in tissue paper and store in a warm, dark, dry place.

To extend the life of the pomander and increase its fragrance, dip it in a mixture of 60g (2tbls) orris root powder and 15g (1tsp) cinnamon or cinnamon and nutmeg. Work the powder well into the surface, until fully coated.

In about three weeks, when the pomander is fully dried, you can add a decorative ribbon, with trails for hanging the pomander in a cupboard.

79

Making a 'lollipop tree'

*Use a container, such as a
flowerpot, as a base. Line the
pot with kitchen paper, to
prevent cracking, before half-
filling with quick-setting
plaster, such as plaster of Paris.
Hold the trunk of the tree in
position.*

*Place a florist's foam globe on
the trunk, and camouflage it
with dried moss held in place
with short wires bent into hair-
pin shapes.*

*Insert a selection of dried
flowers and grasses into the
globe. Helichrysum, sea
lavender and bleached hair
grass are shown here.*

wort or poppy seed heads. Sit the pomander
on a small mound of mastic, then work your way
round, using quick drying glue to fix the flowers
or seed heads in position.

Making Cones and Globes

'Lollipop' and conical trees are relatively
expensive to buy ready made, because they
are so fashionable and because they are time
consuming to do. They are not at all difficult,
though, and an easy project for the novice.

Foundations Florist's foam shapes are perfect
foundations, though you can roughly shape
small cones or globes from rectangular blocks
of florist's foam. This is cheaper, and may be
your only option towards the end of the
Christmas season, as pre-formed shapes
quickly sell out. Any minor irregularities in the
shape are concealed as long as the dried
material does not hug the surface.

You can also use wire netting, packed with
moss. To form a small mesh cone, cut a quarter-
circle shape; make the radii slightly longer than
the desired height of the cone, minus any stem.
Roll the mesh into a cone, overlapping the two
edges, and wire together. A globe is harder to
project on a flat surface. Use a mesh rectangle,
at least twice as long as the desired circumference of the globe. Shape the mesh into a rough
globe.

Reinforce a florist's foam cone or globe with a
wire mesh netting cover if the dried material is
heavy – wired pine cones, for example – or
exceptionally long stemmed. For large-scale
displays, use several blocks of florist's foam,
roughly cut to form the desired shape, and held
together with a tight wrapping of wire netting.

The size of the display is governed by the
size of the foundation, but also depends on the
length of the material used. A cone or globe can
support displays two or three times its diameter, although the longer the stems, the more
material is needed to conceal the foundation.

Bases A base should be strong and stable
enough to support the display, and complement its style. Tiny containers supporting large
displays look odd and can tip over; too large a
container makes the latter look mean. The
width of the container should generally be

between half and the full width of the finished 'tree'. You can do the mechanics in a small container, such as a glass jar or plastic flower pot, then conceal it in a larger, more decorative container.

For a permanent base, you can use a flower pot or decorative pot, filled with quick-setting plaster. Half-fill the container with plaster mixed to a creamy consistency, then insert the trunk so that it touches the container base. Check that it is vertical, add more plaster, leaving 1-2.5cm (½-1in) between the plaster and the rim of the container. Hold the trunk in position until it is self supporting, this will only be a matter of minutes.

Tightly packed sphagnum moss or florist's foam is fine for small, light-weight cones or globes. You can use wickerwork containers, and the foundations can easily be removed, if you want to re-use the container. Light-weight containers filled with moss or florist's foam can tip over; a layer of gravel at the bottom helps. Sand is sometimes used, but it is messy to handle.

A stemmed goblet makes an instant base particularly suitable for a florist's foam cone. Either impale it firmly onto the rim, or, if you are forming a cone from a rectangular block, push it into the goblet and cut the sides of the cone so they extend upwards from the rim.

Trunks Most 'trees' have trunks made of dowels, bamboo canes or broom handles. For a more natural-looking effect, use sections of tree branch, such as birch or tough herbaceous stems, such as nipplewort, or gypsophila. (When cutting a stem, allow extra for it to extend deeply into the base below and the shaped form above.)

Multi-stemmed trunks, made of a forked branch or stem, or two or three branches close together in a base, are attractive. Cones can be stemless, like a Christmas tree clothed to the ground with foliage, but it is easier to work if there is a trunk, and the finished result is usually more elegant.

The floral design can be random, built-up textures; a series of rows on concentric rings; or rings spiralling outwards and downwards from the top. Whatever material you choose, have a generous supply; floral cones and globes need dense covering, or they look skimpy.

Seed heads, nuts and cones are particularly effective, on their own or with flowers. If you are using seed heads, pods and so on in formal rings or spirals, work from small to large down a cone, and to the middle of a globe, reversing the order towards the bottom. Tightly packed pine cones create little spaces between them; fill with moss, nipplewort or perennial sea lavender. The latter has the natural look of miniature conifer branches.

Never allow florist's foam to show, especially the underside of a cone or globe. You can cover the globe or cone with a thin layer of dried moss, fixed with short wires bent into hair-pin shapes, before inserting the stems. Or cover the foundation with a layer of overlapping glycerined beech leaves, though you may have to make small holes with a pin before inserting delicate-stemmed material.

Turn the cone or globe round and round as you progress, to avoid obvious lopsidedness, although minor asymmetry can be an asset. Avoid a heavy, clumsy look by extending occasional twiglets or longer grasses beyond the general shape to break the outline, especially the bottom rim of cones.

A base of plaster or florist's foam needs a cosmetic finish, whether gravel, pebbles, bun or sphagnum moss, or flower heads repeating those used in the main display. If there is an outer, decorative container, fill the space between that and the inner one with sphagnum moss or scrunched up newspaper, then treat the surface as a unified whole.

A large conifer cone can make a miniature tree. Drill a hole in the base, insert a thin dowel with a dab of quick-drying glue on the end, and insert the other end into a suitable container. (Old-fashioned terra cotta 'thumb' pots, used for growing on seedlings are ideal.) Display a 'forest' of these tiny trees on a dining-table, or use them singly for individual place settings. Also try water plantain (*Alisma plantago aquatica*) which has the conical shape of a Christmas tree, but is airier and more delicate, the flowers, and seed pods that follow, are carried in decreasing whorls up the stem.

Breaking the rigid outline of a cone or globe can give it a bit of character. Here gypsophila, quaking grass, hare's tail grass and long, pink rat's tail statice are allowed to arch, hang or even droop at will.

81

Styles of Arrangement

The wreaths, swags and garlands that are so much a part of the Christmas scene are covered on pages 74, 75, and 111, respectively, but many other imaginative possibilites exist. For a sophisticated Christmas tree, forego the usual silver balls and angels and hang miniature wicker baskets filled with potpourri, lavender blossom, and little flower heads. You can economize by filling each basket nearly up to the rim with tightly packed tissue paper, then covering it with a thin layer of the chosen dried material. Use extravagant raffia bows or narrow ribbons to attach the baskets to the tree. Or entwine the tree with a looped garland of braided raffia, studded with dried flowers.

Little presents are part of Christmas hospitability. Fill a gold-sprayed basket with potpourri of red rose petals, then hide small presents, lucky-dip style, inside. Extend long, thin ribbons of red and gold from each present to trail over the edge of the basket. It would make a lovely dining-table centre-piece, with a ribbon leading to each place setting.

Christmas Decorations

Artificial Christmas trees conjure up images of awkward, sparse looking limbs and bright-green plastic foliage. 'Artificial' Christmas trees composed of dried material can be as beautiful as your imagination allows. Cover florist's foam cones or globes with a thin layer of quick-drying glue, then press on sphagnum moss, to form a miniature Christmas tree. Stud with tiny silver balls, thin red ribbon bows, or bright-red glixia flowers. For children, wire up wrapped boiled sweets in red, white and candy-striped colours, and attach them to the tree or pile them, like miniature presents, at its base.

Fresh box clippings have a long lifespan, especially if kept in a cool room. Use them instead of moss, to cover cones or globes; remove a few of the lowest leaves, and insert the stems directly into the florist's foam. Decor-

A pair of sophisticated Christmas wreaths made from modest ingredients. The willow ring, far left, is shown being made on page 75; pheasant tail feathers, free from a kindly butcher, and sequin-waste bows, add the finishing touches. The alder wreath, left, has an entirely different character, more intricate and formal. The black alder branches are built up round a wire ring, then given several light coats of gold spray paint. Gold-painted nuts and red-dyed achillea form the decorations.

ate with dried flowers, as above; silver- or gold sprayed safflower (*Carthamus*) make instant mini-tree decorations and their stiff stems can be stuck directly into the florist's foam. Inexpensive gold chains or ropes of rhinestones or fake pearls, bought from costume jewellery counters, make ideal garlands for miniature moss trees. The naturalness and matt finish of the moss subdues the frankly fake, glittery quality of the 'jewels'. Sales are ideal hunting grounds; the chains, of course, can be used forever.

Dwarf conifers are among the most popular of garden plants. As a gift for a gardening enthusiast or for your own garden, you could buy one and decorate it with sprigs of dried gypsophila and rose buds, tied with ribbon bows. Keep the tree in a cool spot until Christmas eve, then use it to decorate the home on Christmas day, before planting it out. Its plastic or whalehide pot can be sprayed gold for the occasion; a terra cotta pot is too nice to embellish.

The traditional symbols of Christmas can be reinterpreted in dried material. Particularly popular in America are the red-and-white-striped candy canes. Take an old walking stick or pair of walking sticks, and cover, as above with a thin layer of glue and sphagnum moss. When dry, run a red ribbon, with tiny dabs of glue on the underside, diagonally up each cane. Finish with a big red bow, and cluster of silver balls, if wished.

Father Christmas, or Santa Claus, can pull a sledge filled with dried flowers. Inexpensive plastic reindeer can be covered with a thin coat of glue and sphagnum moss pressed on, as above. Herds or individual deer can 'wander' under a Christmas tree or across a dining-table. For children, snowmen can be made of three florist's foam globes in diminishing sizes, and covered with white delphinium florets, wired into little sprigs.

Christmas can provide the antidote, or at least the excuse, to transform a tired or faded dried flower display. A spray tin of silver, gold, bronze, copper or glossy red paint is all that is needed, and a few sprigs of conifer inserted after spraying, or tiny metallic balls nestling in the centre, can reinforce the Christmas theme.

Three little table-top trees take their cues from Christmas. The tiny conifer, right, is built up on a larch branch, with tightly wired bunches of dyed green broom bloom forming the foliage. Gold-sprayed conifer cones stud the cone, and a sequin-waste pleated circle adorns the top.

The red-and-white 'Christmas tree' centre, is built up on a stemmed wine glass. The foliage is an evenly dense coating of bleached hare's tail grass, white anaphalis and dyed red anaphalis. The lollipop tree, extreme right, is built on a stem of cow parsley. The topmost globe is made of a florist's foam globe, covered with gold-sprayed acorn cups and beech mast, and studded with fake pearls. The middle-sized globe is simply a leek flower head, and the lowest globe is a shell-encrusted souvenir from a coastal resort. Gold-sprayed hydrangea hides the florist's foam base.

Easy Gifts

With dried flowers, almost anything qualifies as a gift, providing you can carry it without damage. Determining factors are the flowers' delicacy and bulk, rather than weight. Another determining factor is, of course, the recipient. Some people would prefer a bouquet to arrange at leisure; others would like a ready-made display. Some people have small homes in which space is at a premium; others have huge corners to spare and would welcome an armful of dried flowers. And although sexual equality is becoming an accepted part of daily life, some men, and most boys, are still embarrassed by receiving flowers, and another gift would be more appropriate.

The third factor is the occasion; if you can relate the flowers or container, or both, to the particular event, it makes a more memorable, and perhaps useful, present. For welcoming a new baby, the most dramatic gift would be a wicker bassinet or Moses basket filled with dried flowers, either in the traditional colours of pink for a girl and blue for a boy, or in a less traditional scheme. (Dried gypsophila and pink or blue delphinium would make a good filler; there are several shades of pinks and blues available, although they may need to be ordered specially.)

On a smaller scale try a woven, lidded wicker basket filled with dried flowers; eventually, the basket can be used for keeping all the accoutrements normally associated with a baby: talcum powder, baby oil, tissues, and so on. Most traditional of all would be a wickerwork or ceramic stork, filled with dried flowers; 'storks' are sold at florists and speciality shops.

Dolls' furniture, such as rocking chairs, cradles or trunks can form the receptacle for dried flowers, to make 'double' presents. Dolls' furniture varies from beautiful but inexpensive wickerwork and bamboo, imported from the Orient, to exquisitely handcrafted and expensive collectors' pieces, in the style of Chippendale, Sheraton and so on. Again, match the furniture to the recipient; there are many adults for whom a handmade piece of dolls' furniture would be most welcome.

A house-warming present could combine the beauty of dried flowers and the practicality of, say, a piece of kitchen equipment. A French wire tiered egg basket could contain little posies of dried flowers in each holder; or a beautiful soup ladle have a decorative spray of dried flowers fixed to the neck of a handle. A small wooden wine rack could contain, not wine, but tightly packed bunches of dried flowers, ready for arranging. A long, thin French bread basket would not need many dried flowers to fill it, and could start life as a table decoration before filling its eventual purpose. Or, for someone collecting a particular china pattern, a cup and saucer or soup bowl could contain a toning posy of dried flowers. And for a keen cook, a wreath of herbs or dried garlic (see pages 8-9) would be perfect.

Presents hidden within presents always have an Aladdin-like charm, and are great fun to open. Something as mundane as a lidded cooking pot or opaque storage jar, containing potpourri, would become doubly valuable. On a more luxurious note, a piece of jewellery or bottle of perfume nestling within a little box of potpourri makes for an attractive, fragrant presentation.

Quick and easy presents for decorating a wall can be made of dried flowers and oriental fans. These are inexpensive and come in a range of sizes and shapes. Plain ones of bamboo, woven wickerwork or palm leaf are best. A small posy can be wired to the handle, or dried material fanned out to mirror the shape of its backdrop; if more time and skill is available, a wired, crescent-shaped spray could adorn one side.

For hospital patients, dried-flower displays are especially suitable, as the water in vases of fresh flowers has been found to be a breeding ground for bacteria, as well as a source of odour. And because hospitals have a particular antiseptic smell, dried flowers that can provide fragrance are always welcome. Potpourri or lavender in a potpourri pot would be powerful long after the usual fresh freesias and lilies fade. An old-fashioned, monogrammed lawn and lace handkerchief, tied with a narrow ribbon, could serve as an alternative receptacle, and could be used when the potpourri or lavender eventually loses its fragrance.

Tiny, flower-filled dolls' house furniture, a flower-festooned gift basket, and a potpourri-filled Victorian dish are presents made memorable by the addition of dried flowers.

Roses and Valentine's day are inextricably linked. Here, the present is twofold; a charming cluster of roses and sea lavender in an old-fashioned china basket.

The ultimate in Valentine's Day gifts: a huge, dried flower heart for hanging on a wall. A florist's foam heart shape forms the foundation, and a mixture of hydrangea flowers, pink helichrysum and pink-dyed anaphalis, gypsophila, pink and white larkspur florets and safflower buds form the bulk of the display. A cluster of pink rose buds and pink-dyed hair grass provides the central focal point.

Valentine's Day

It is a fact of life that most flowers are given by men to women on this occasion, and most men do not arrange dried flowers. However, Valentine's Day dinners or parties may require floral decorations, and romantic displays can be made, without any personal connotations, for a feminine-looking bedroom or living-room.

Valentine's Day has no direct connection with its namesakes, two martyred bishops, and although February 14th was chosen by the Victorians as the day to exchange Valentine cards because birds were said to pair for the year on that day, this, too, is untrue. It is more likely that Valentine's Day has its roots in ancient pagan rites. Nonetheless, Valentine's Day remains a conveniently ritualized outlet for expressing romance, with the full blessing of commerce.

Red roses and hearts are the two recurrent symbols of Valentine's Day. (The forget-me-nots and lilies-of-the-valley that adorned most Victorian Valentine's Day cards have fallen out of favour.) Easiest of all is a bunch of a dozen dried red roses, tied with a toning ribbon bow. Most red roses darken dramatically when dried, so the usual cherry-red florist's ribbon makes

red roses look dirty; a pink, white or deep maroon ribbon is a wiser choice. Pink roses hold their colour better when dried.

Heart-shaped florist's foam bases can be decorated as for wreaths (see page 74), using flowers in shades of red and pink; heart-shaped bases may have to be ordered specially. A wire coat hanger can be shaped into a heart, then covered with sphagnum moss and decorated with flowers and tiny ribbon bows (see page 74). There are many heart-shaped covered boxes and baskets, in porcelain, china, brass, wickerwork and woven bamboo, which can be filled with potpourri. Open baskets, and heart-shaped moulds available from kitchen shops, can be filled with florist's foam cut to fit, and an arrangement, based on pink or red, built up from the base.

Traditional heart-shaped boxes of chocolate often come pre-decorated with unmemorable cloth or plastic flowers. These can be replaced with a cluster of dried flowers. Again, it is pointless to try to match the cherry red of Valentine chocolate boxes with red flowers, and pink or white might be better, but a gold paper box makes an impressive setting for deep red dried roses.

A florist's foam globe, either hanging from a ribbon or in the form of a little tree, would make an unusual Valentine present, densely covered with pink helichrysum, globe amaranth, campion and dyed material, such as pink hare's tail grass and quaking grass. Reindeer moss is available in several dyed colours, including pink, but it is phenomenally expensive, and would probably have to be ordered in large quantities. The natural grey-green of undyed reindeer moss makes a pleasantly neutral background for pinks and reds, and in no way diminishes the romantic appearance of the gift.

The chubby, cherub-like, idealized children that feature in Renaissance painting and sculpture, also feature in the imagery of Valentine's Day, as does Cupid himself. A centre-piece for a Valentine's Day dinner-party could be a traditional china cherub vase, overflowing with dried pink paeonies or huge, old-fashioned pink or red garden roses.

Modern Arrangements

Categorizing types of flower arrangements, like categorizing people, usually involves oversimplification, and can be counter-productive in the end. Many so-called modern arrangements share attributes with traditional formal arrangements; both depend on clear, uncluttered outline and dense mass, and both share a potential anonymity that can result from rigid adherence to geometry. Other modern arrangements, particularly abstract, linear ones, are more akin to traditional oriental displays, containing a minimum of material, chosen for its perfect form and symbolic content, and asymmetrically balanced. Some people attribute the adjective 'modern' to any floral display they do not quite understand, rather like modern music.

Ingredients and Containers Certain types of dried plant material are inherently modern looking: alder, contorted willow and hazel, for example, and bulrushes, driftwood and dried bamboo. It may be because they have clearly defined outlines, or because they are more linear than massive, but they do have an instantly recognizable modern feel. This does not mean that they are unsuitable for traditional displays, but simply that using them, particularly on their own, is a foolproof way to achieve a modern look. Of the dried flowers: proteas, craspedias, banksias and stirlingias somehow look more modern than garden roses, larkspur and helichrysums.

Likewise modern containers: a stark glass cylinder, or stainless steel cube, filled with a floating mass of gypsophila or love-lies bleeding is unmistakably modern. The setting in which the floral display is seen is equally important and can reinforce or contradict modernity. (Changing a setting is easier to achieve in the fantasy world of a photographic studio than in real life!)

A flower arrangement becomes modern as much by how material is used as by the type of material chosen. Delicate easy fillers, such as gypsophila or lady's mantle, can unite disparate flowers in a haze of soft colour, and somehow make a coherent whole out of a basically incoherent arrangement, but they do

not impart modernity in this fashion. Used on their own, as described above, or with absolute, sculptural conviction, they take on modern overtones. For example, an Elizabethan-type ruff of tightly packed lady's mantle at the base of a mass of vertical, green bells of Ireland.

Flowers and flower arrangements are traditionally feminine, both symbolically and in ordinary usage. Most modern arrangements, however, lack this feminine softness and are, instead, startling, thought provoking, humorous or even overwhelming. Like the difference between modern and traditional sculptures, modern floral arrangements challenge the eyes and the mind, rather than restfully confirm what we already know.

There are no rules governing modern floral displays, only general guidelines. 'Less is more' might be the main one: less elaboration, less varied material and less fussiness. This is balanced by more clarity, more simplicity, more decisiveness, more streamlining and more emphasis on the quality or form of individual flowers or other components of the display. And perhaps, in the end, more thrill in achieving success.

Bleached poppy seed heads, galax leaves and achillea are mixed with the natural colours of lotus seed head, helichrysum and protea calyx, for an austerely modern display.

Contorted willow, far left, is the most obvious choice for an instant, large scale and impressive modern display. Clusters of dried echinops heads add interest at the base of the branches, and the marble geometric objects complete the group.

SPRING

Even the most devoted dried-flower arranger cannot ignore the glory of fresh flowers in spring: the bunches of cheap daffodils, tulips and narcissi that fill flower shops and stalls, and the tiny posies of violets that are sold nestling in their own heart-shaped leaves. This is material that deserves to be displayed directly and simply, so its very freshness can shine out. However, some spring flowers, such as primrose, polyanthus and hyacinth, can be preserved in a desiccant, for use at a more barren time of the year, but with most, the pleasure is immediate and short lived.

In spite of a temporary (and understandable) shift in loyalty, there is much to be done with dried material at this time of the year. Spring means spring cleaning, and dried flower displays that have withstood the rigours of life indoors for the past six months usually need attention. Broken or damaged flowers should be removed and repaired or discarded, and their positions filled with replacement material, whether exact replicas or something entirely different. Alternatively, displays could be taken apart and stored until the autumn or the floral constituents rearranged in a completely new way.

For those with a garden, spring means sowing hardy annuals, including a good proportion of everlastings, or immortelles, to provide dried material for next autumn and winter. And open to all is the lovely option of woodland walks in pursuit of mosses for fresh- or dried-flower miniature moss gardens.

In the Shops

Gilding the lily is always a temptation, and to some people, the less done to dried flowers, the better. There are, however, occasions when selective use of floral cosmetics can improve a display or give it a particular relevance. Faded flowers and seed pods, for example, can be given a new look for any festivity by being sprayed silver, gold, red or any other suitable colour. And though it is hard to gift wrap a dried flower arrangement, it is easy to tie a ribbon bow onto the handle of a basket, or tape it to the side of a bowl. (Once the ribbon loses its pristine freshness, it can be detached and discarded or replaced.) Using dried flowers creatively is often related to interior decoration, and painting containers to match the decor of a room offers many possibilities. On a more technical level, clear varnishes and sprays can help keep delicate, fluffy seed heads intact.

Buying Ribbons, Paints and Varnishes
The plastic, acetate or paper-based ribbons used by most florists are sold on spools of various widths and colours. The ribbon is stiff and crisp looking, identical on both sides and can be formed into upstanding loops. Corkscrew-like, trailing curls can be made by pulling the ribbon tightly over a scissor blade. Some wide ribbons can be torn lengthways, into narrower widths without fraying, thus eliminating the need for several spools of the same colour. Florist's ribbons are also available in pre-cut lengths, with end tabs which, when pulled, concertina the ribbon into a perfect, multi-looped bow, complete with trails.

Florist's ribbons are available from wholesale suppliers, stationers, gift shops and specialist craft stores, and some florists may sell them. From the florist's point of view, such ribbons are perfect: inexpensive, waterproof and foolproof. From the aesthetic point of view, however, they can have an over-shiny appearance, and some of the strong colours can look unnatural, compared to the subtle colouring of dried material.

Haberdashers are more fertile hunting grounds. Polyester satin ribbon, in various colours and widths ranging from 2mm-7.5cm ($\frac{1}{16}$-3in) is good for general work, although the bows tend to be more flaccid than those of florist's ribbons. Polyester grosgrain, nylon and woven-edge velvet are alternatives. Heavily patterned ribbons should be used with care, although self stripes, dots or picot edging can be quite successful. Depending on the container and style of the display, gold and silver braids, narrow satin cords, various thicknesses of curtain cord, and, from knitting shops, soft wool, such as mohair or angora, are possibilities. End-of-season sales can yield lovely finds in both haberdashers and wool shops; ends-of-dye lots, odd skeins or balls and short lengths of ribbon.

Using two narrow strips of contrasting ribbon or wool, or a mixture of the two, can give a more delicate look than a single, wide ribbon. Using small, narrow bows on wires inserted into the florist's foam can have the effect of butterflies, floating above the display. If the container is a loosely woven one, interweaving narrow strands of toning ribbon or wool; or tacking a ruffled band of *broderie anglaise* or lace to the rim, can add a personal touch.

Plaited or twisted raffia, knotted at the ends, can be used like ribbon, for an informal effect, perhaps with a few flowers or pods tucked in. Large, bright cotton calico or silk handkerchiefs can be folded diagonally and knotted in the middle, to look like bows, and can be used after the display has faded. Ready made bows in a variety of fabrics are also available from hair care counters of drug stores, chemists, department stores and larger supermarkets. These are ideal for instant, professional-looking decorations for a dried flower gift.

There is little point in attempting to re-create the saturated colouring of commercially dyed dried flowers, such as dyed glixia or anaphalis, because commercial plant dyes are not normally available and special processes are involved. Adding a water-soluble dye, such as artist's drawing inks, to glycerine when preserving pale material – bells of Ireland or eucalyptus, for example – can give contrasting veined effects.

Many shops and fabric departments are a superb hunting ground for ribbons to enhance dried flower displays. Ribbons offer enormous potential for personalizing or adding colour to a dried flower display, but they can never rescue a boring or sloppy arrangement.

External application of paint is more common, and spray paints are the easiest to apply, especially to fragile or intricate flowers and seed pods. High gloss, semi-gloss and matt finishes are available, in a range of colours. High gloss, quick-drying car spray paints are particularly good. The disadvantages of spray paint are its cost and inevitable wastage; the nozzle must be 25-30cm (10-12in) away from the object, to avoid drips, and a lot of paint ends up on the surrounding newspaper. According to the number of applications, density can range from light to opaque, allowing the natural colours to predominate. Several light coats are more effective than one heavy one; allow the paint to dry for two or three minutes between applications. A single light coat of metallic spray is a more subtle way of giving an arrangement a Christmas feel than glitter. Less expensive, ready-mixed tins of metallic paint and metallic powder, in gold, silver, bronze and copper shades, for mixing with an oil-based liquid, are also available.

Large, sturdy material, such as hazel or birch branches, or milkweed pods, can be painted or dipped in emulsion diluted with water. If you rest them on newspaper to dry, turn them over from time to time, to prevent the paint forming a blob and sticking the pod to the paper. If you have painted a room, and there is left-over paint, use it to colour-coordinate inexpensive woven baskets. Great fun can be had with paint left over from stippling, rag rolling or marbling walls. Inexpensive, tiny tester pots of paint are available from paint stores and DIY centres. There are various wood stains available, for colouring decorative wood, although bleached driftwood is most attractive in its natural form. Lastly, try using poster paint powder to give a temporary toning tint to containers.

Polyurethane spray can give an attractive, subtle sheen to pine cones, nuts and dark seed pods, such as those of baptisia. Artist's clear varnish can also be used, but a high gloss can sometimes be counterproductive. In extremes, hair lacquer or clear nail varnish will keep clematis seed heads intact. Whatever the type of paint, the surface of the material to be treated should be dry, clean and dirt free.

Bluebells, lawn daisies and buttercups in an alpine meadow in spring may seem completely remote from dried flowers. Buttercups, however, can be hung up to dry, as can lawn daisies, either with or without their petals (Choose long-stemmed specimens, if possible.) The round, fat seed pods that follow the bluebell flowers are worth collecting before fully ripe and hanging upside down to dry.

In the Garden

Sowing annuals directly where they are to flower is easier than starting seeds off under glass, and less equipment is needed. On the other hand, you have less control of the environment – weather, birds, soil pests, and so on – and germination can be patchy. For this reason, some people prefer to sow even hardy annuals under glass (see pages 63-64) although a few, such as helipterums, cannot be transplanted and must be sown *in situ*. The soil requirements are the same as those for half-hardy annuals (see page 64), but ideally, you should wait a week or two after applying fertilizer before sowing, to avoid scorching the seedlings.

Start sowing in April, weather permitting; you can also sow some half-hardy annuals outdoors, but leave them until the end of the month or the beginning of May. Most hardy annuals prefer full sun but some, such as love-in-a-mist, tolerate light shade. Just before sowing, work the surface to a fine tilth. Firm down the soil with your feet, then go backwards and forwards over it with a metal rake, until the soil is evenly crumbly. (Do not make it too fine, or it will cake solid after the first heavy rainfall, creating an impenetrable hard pan!) Seeds need a steady supply of water to germinate, so if the soil is dry, water thoroughly before sowing, using a fine rose on a watering can or garden hose adjusted to a fine spray.

How to Sow
You can sow annuals in rows, vegetable-garden style, but they will look more attractive if broadcast in irregularly shaped patches. Use silver sand to mark out individual patches, making them interlapping in the way that crazy paving, or crocodile skin, does. Most of the tallest growing material should be at the back of a border or bed, if it faces one way, or in the centre, if it is an island bed. Bring some of the tall plants forward, though, to break a potentially regimented outline.

To get an even distribution of small seed, mix it with silver sand first, and sprinkle it, like

salt, from the palm of your hand. Slightly larger seeds can be tapped out of the packet, but tap the first few into your hand, until you get it exactly right. Seeds large enough to handle can be sown individually, but if you want a decorative effect, avoid sowing in straight lines. With naturally large and pelleted seeds, sow at their final spacings; thinning is unnecessary.

If sowing in rows, use a garden line to get them straight, and a Dutch or draw hoe to make a shallow, v-shaped drill. The smaller the seed, the shallower the depression; tiny poppy seeds need the merest furrow, while sunflower seeds should be planted 5cm (2in) deep. Try to make the depth even all along the row, or germination will be patchy. If you are broadcast sowing, firmly draw a rake over the soil surface, to make a series of criss-crossed small furrows.

After sowing, cover the seeds with their own depth of fine, crumbly soil or, in the case of tiny seed, sifted sand. Draw the little mounds of soil either side of seed drills back over them, to infill, leaving the finished surface level. Label the rows or patches, and water, again with a fine mist, if the weather is dry.

Planting out Half-hardy Annuals

At the end of April or beginning of May, there is often a spell of convincingly summery weather, and it is tempting to plant out half-hardy annuals then. This is usually followed, unfortunately, by late spring frost, which can kill or stunt young plants, and waste a season's growth. Wait until the last week in May or first week in June, depending on local weather conditions. If you are buying half-hardy annuals from garden centres, let them take the risk with the weather.

Moving half-hardy annuals from the comforts of indoors to the rigours of outdoor life, at a single stroke, can be fatal. In late April or early May, start hardening them off by gradually exposing them to more light and ventilation, but protecting them from frost. Those grown in a cold frame can have the frame lights gradually opened wider and wider, during successive days, but closed at nights or whenever frost threatens. Cover the lights with sacking or newspaper if there is heavy frost. Most people do not have cold frames, in which case place

the trays or pots out in a sunny spot, sheltered from east winds, during the day, and bring them indoors, somewhere cool but frost free, in the evenings or if bad weather threatens. In gardening folklore, grey mornings followed by clearing afternoon skies mean night frosts, so be prepared. Plants being hardened off still need regular watering and applications of dilute liquid fertilizer.

After the last frost, plant out; the sooner the better. Most annuals, especially everlastings prefer a sunny spot, with a light, free-draining soil not overly rich and definitely weed free. Ideally, it should have been dug over the previous autumn or winter; if not, dig it over now, removing any stones or debris as you go. Incorporate a 5cm (2in) layer of damp peat, and firm with your feet, to level the soil. Give a very light application of a low nitrogen content fertilizer plus superphosphate, starvation is as bad as overly rich conditions.

Choose a warm day, but wait until evening before planting, to reduce water loss and the risk of wilting. Water the root balls thoroughly, and the ground, unless it is already damp. (Check with a spade first; you may find the first half inch or so of topsoil wet and dark, and underneath that bone dry.)

Plants grown in peat pots or pellets can be planted directly into the soil; remove those grown in individual plastic or clay pots by turning the pots upside down, using your spread-out fingers to contain the root ball. Gently lever out those grown in trays, keeping as much of the roots intact as possible; a kitchen fork or plastic seed label is helpful.

Using a trowel, make the hole generously wide and deep, and place the root ball so that its upper surface is the same level, or slightly deeper than, the surrounding soil. Cover with soil, then firm with a trowel or your fist, and check afterwards by tugging at a leaf. If the plant is pulled out, begin again.

Spacing for individual species is given on seed packets – always save these – but you can generally space them a little closer than recommended, as they are grown as a crop, not specimen plants. Love-lies-bleeding, when crowded, produces finer, more delicate spikes, which are useful for any small-scale displays.

If you have cloches, protect the young plants for the first few nights after planting out; if faced with an unexpected frost, a single sheet of newspaper resting on the plants is often enough protection. If the weather is dry immediately after planting out, water generously; after a couple of weeks, the plants should be established enough not to need watering, except in exceptionally dry weather. Be on the look out for rogue weeds, and remove as necessary.

Choosing Plants for Drying

Very few people build their whole garden around the concept of providing material for dried arrangements. For most people, a garden is meant to be an attractive setting for the house and a pleasant space for relaxing outdoors. However, there are many perennial herbaceous, bulbous and woody plants, and even edible plants, that contribute to the visual success of the garden and provide good material for preserving. Although flowers first spring to mind, it is often the plants that provide foliage or seed heads that best serve the needs of the garden and the flower arranger in equal measure.

Interesting foliage for dried arrangements is more difficult to buy than flowers, and easier, once a plant is mature, to harvest without creating any noticeable gaps in the garden. Any of the plants suitable for glycerining (see page 135-137) are worth growing. Particularly tolerant of shade or less-than-perfect growing conditions are Mexican orange blossom (*Choisya ternata*), various species and cultivars of elaeagnus, mahonia and spotted laurel (*Aucuba japonica*). (When preserved with glycerine, the spotted laurel mercifully loses its spots and becomes a rich, browny black.) If you do not like the somewhat Victorian and grim overtones often associated with the spotted laurel, try the variety 'Longifolia', with long, narrow, bright-green leaves. It is a female form, and to have berries as well as handsome foliage, plant at least one of its male counterpart, 'Lance Leaf', with similarly narrow, unspotted leaves.

Although common laurel (*Prunus laurocerasus*) is widely available and takes well to preserving with antifreeze, the leaves are quite massive and difficult to use in small or delicate arrangements. Again, there are named varieties worth growing with smaller leaves, more elegant in small arrangements. 'Otto Luyken' is low and spreading, with horizontal-growing branches and narrow, tapered leaves, less than 2.5cm (1in) wide. 'Zabelliana' has graceful, willowy leaves. (Both of these are more suitable for small gardens than the common laurel.) You may have to go to specialist nurseries to obtain these varieties, but, as the shrubs live for many years, the extra time and effort is minimal by comparison. Portuguese laurel (*Prunus lusitanica*) has attractive shiny foliage, rather like an evergreen version of ornamental cherry foliage. It takes both pruning and glycerining well, and lacks the somewhat clumsy look of common laurel.

For full sun, brooms and silvery plants are ideal. Artemisias, particularly A. *absinthum*, A. 'Silver Queen', and A. 'Lambrook Silver'; B*allota pseudodictamnus*; and horehound, M*arrubium vulgare*, provide material suitable for drying. Although neither B*allota pseudodictamnus* nor hore-hound is particularly impressive, both have reliably dense, bushy growth and attractive, bract-covered stems. Lamb's tongue (*Stachys lanata*) comes in non-flowering and flowering forms. If you grow the flowering form, you can cut the gracefully twisting stems just as they start to flower and hang them upside-down to dry. The hardy perennial pearl everlasting (*Anaphalis triplinervis*) is another good subject, strong growing in the garden and long lasting once dried; for smaller gardens try the similar but more compact A. *nubigena*. Unlike most other silvery plants, pearl everlastings tolerate light shade and slightly moist soil. In common with other silver-leaved plants, however, they cannot tolerate long periods of cold and wet conditions.

Lady's mantle (*Alchemilla mollis*), B*ergenia cordifolia* and larger sedums do first-class service in the garden, and provide foliage for preserving. (Float bergenia foliage in a glycerine solution.) Hosta foliage can be air dried, or dried in a small amount of water, and its natural curves

*The unfortunately named stinking iris (*Iris foetidissima*) above, has dull little flowers, but is worth growing for the sake of its brilliant orange-red berries, which dry easily. Pick before the pods are fully open.*

used to add a sculptural quality to a dried display. The tiny greeny-yellow flowers of lady's mantle, and reddy brown ones of sedums, also air dry beautifully. Other perennials worth growing for their flowers include achillea, tansy, acanthus, goldenrod, knapweed, astrantia, astilbe, sea thrift and sea holly, delphinium, echinops, blazing stars (Liatris), gypsophila and veronicas. Like annual statice (*Limonium sinuatum*), perennial statice (L. *latifolium*) is attractive and easy to dry, but so widely available commercially that it is not worth growing specifically to dry. A particular challenge to dry are paeonies; the single and semi-double ones are easier than the fully double varieties, and desiccant is the best technique.

Carefully consider plants with attractive seed heads. You then get the full measure of a floral display, and the seed heads as crops for drying. Species tend to be more rewarding in this respect than hybrids, which are often sterile. Again, a horticultural compromise is necessary, as seed heads unwanted for propagation are normally snapped off as soon as they start to form, to prevent the plant wasting energy and encourage it to build up reserves for the following year's display. This is probably more vital for a young plant, while becoming established, than a well established one.

Garden plants with particularly pretty seed pods include columbine; campion; foxgloves, hollyhocks and species iris, especially I. *sibirica*, I. *japonica*, I. *pseudacorus* and the so-called stinking iris, I. *foetidissima*. (The seeds of the stinking iris are a brilliant orange red.) Species tulips have pale tan, tripartite seed cases, and alliums and grape hyacinths also have attractive seed cases. Paeonies allowed to set seed produce attractive shiny seed cases, containing seeds ranging from red and black to fuchsia pink and blue. Lupins, and the lupin-like false indigo (*Baptisia australis*) are worth growing for the pea-like seed pods that follow the flowers; those of the false indigo are a rich chocolate brown. Montbretia (*Crocosmia*) and the similar-looking Aunt Eliza (*Curtonus paniculatus*) have twin rows of seed cases on gracefully arching stems, plus spiky foliage that dries superbly.

Poppy seed heads, with their flat, ribbed lids, are too well known to need description. The star-shaped seed pods of the gas plant (*Dictamnus albus*) look like brown flowers and are densely carried on the large spikes. (The common name comes from the flammable gas given off by the flowers' oil glands.) Unfortunately, the much loved Chinese lantern (*Physalis alkekengii*) has insignificant white flowers and a rather dishevelled habit of growth, and is ideally consigned to an out-of-the-way patch of ground. St John's wort follows its charming yellow flowers with rich-brown, flower-shaped seed cases. *Hypericum androsaenum* and H. × *inodorum*, particularly, produce their seed capsules in clusters on long stems, very useful for adding height as well as interest to a display.

Symphoricarpos, or snowberry, is worth growing for its arching sprays of glossy berries, white in most forms but tinged lilac in 'Magic Berry', and tinged pink in 'Mother of Pearl'. They do not dry in the conventional sense, but last for weeks out of water, and when they begin to shrivel can then be discarded and replaced with fresh material, if available.

Vegetables and Herbs

Although most vegetables are grown as annuals, there are a few long-term subjects which can provide material for drying. Leave a few globe artichokes or cardoon flower buds to mature, and use the thistly heads in large-scale displays. Sorrel, the delicious basis of French sorrel soup, is a close cousin of wild dock; allow a few plants to set seed, and harvest the rich russet pods. Rhubarb, if left to its own devices, produces an enormous flower plume, which can be air dried and used in dramatic, large-scale displays. Asparagus foliage can be cut when green and air dried, provided you do not denude the plant and rob it of its next year's energy.

Herbs have been dried for centuries for culinary use, but can also be used in dried flower displays. The leaves of purple sage (*Salvia officinalis* 'Purpurea') are particularly attractive dried; try, too, the yellow variegated 'Icterina' and the more usual garden, grey leaved species. Bay responds well to glycerine, turning a rich deep brown, and becomes pale greeny-brown when air dried. Rosemary air dries well, although the spiky foliage tends to drop at the slightest touch. Rosemary is also an unpredictable shrub, and old, established specimens may suddenly succumb to a bad winter or even to severe pruning. If this happens, carefully dig up the gnarled roots. Clean and bleach them, and use them to add a sculptural quality to dried displays.

Planting

Spring is the traditional time when nurseries and garden centres are fully stocked, awaiting the hoards of weekend browsers and buyers who replenish their gardens then. Although choosing your plants is exciting, planting them is often more laborious. Nonetheless, poor planting is one of the foremost causes of untimely deaths among plants.

Timing It is easier buying plants than planting them, in terms of physical effort. The vast majority of plants are container grown, and can wait a day, or even a few days, for planting without ill effect, so do not set yourself the task of planting, in one go, more than you have the energy or interest to cope with. Do not plant when the ground is frozen or waterlogged, either; leave the plants in a cool but frost-free shed or garage, never in a warm room indoors. Make sure, too, that they are not exposed to drying winds, a particular spring problem. Dormant plants are easier going about this delay than container plants in full growth, which need a steady supply of water and light as near as possible to their permanent positions.

Position With the exception of a few perennial plants, such as paeonies and hellebores, which resent root disturbance, most herbaceous perennials are moveable. Keep in mind the recommended spacing between plants. If they become crowded out by a more vigorous subject, or by their own new growth, or they do not seem to like the position, you can move them, in part or entirely, during the dormant season. Shrubs and trees are less flexible in this respect, and their first siting should be their final one. Therefore, you should allow for their ultimate height and spread in relation to surrounding shrubs and trees. Nearby peren-

nials can be moved, as the long-term subjects increase in size.

Preparing the Ground With perennials, trees and shrubs, making sure the ground is weed free is extremely important, as weeds such as couch grass, ground elder and clover can work themselves well and truly into the roots of the cultivated plants, making eradication virtually impossible.

Whatever the subject, make the planting holes well and truly more generous, in depth and diameter, than the dimensions of the container and root ball. Some soils are compact and hard for roots to penetrate, and if the root ball is rammed into a hole no bigger, or even slightly smaller than itself, failure is almost inevitable. Back fill the dug-out soil, adding well-rotted compost or damp peat and bone-meal, so that the upper surface of the plant's root ball ends up level with the soil.

Watering Water the plant thoroughly, remove it from its container, and place in the centre of the hole. If there are roots growing round and round in a circle at the bottom of the root ball, tease them out before planting. Back fill the space between the root ball and the side of the hole with soil, again working in a bit of rotted compost if possible. Firm the soil as you go, using your fist or the back of a trowel. Finish with an even, level surface.

Plants need plenty of water during their first growing season. If you are planting actively growing material, and the soil is dry, puddle the plants in. Fill the dug-out hole with water, and let it drain away, then plant. Make doubly sure evergreen plants have a steady supply of water, as they need extra time to become established. Check newly planted subjects after frosts, which can lift them, and re-firm if necessary.

As important as having a rich source of material from your own garden is having a network of gardening friends, with whom cuttings can be traded. As with cooking, it is easy to find a combination of ingredients that can be polished to perfection, and become slightly lazy and unadventurous, turning out lovely but repetitious displays season after season. New material is, by its nature, challenging, and is always a good idea to experiment.

Although globe artichokes, are usually grown as a vegetable, they can be impressive in dried flower arrangements. For this purpose, the flower buds must be left on the plant to mature and produce their thistle-like flowers. Pick in autumn and preserve by air drying.

In the Wild

Before the advent of florist's foam, mosses played a far larger role in flower arranging than now. Sphagnum moss, in particular, was a basic part of a florist's wares. Although not particularly attractive, its leaves are made up of hollow cells with tiny pores, so sphagnum moss acts like a sponge, absorbing many times its own weight in water. It can be soaked, then squeezed until the required degree of dampness is reached, and packed round the stems of cut flowers and foliage, to prevent wilting. Wrapped with rose wire or wire netting, damp sphagnum moss formed the basis of fresh wreaths, globes and cones, and the inner core of containers. In dried arrangements, dried sphagnum moss provided camouflage and, in conjunction with wire or netting, support.

Collecting Mosses

Today, moss is used primarily in a decorative role, forming the 'lawns' in miniature gardens and beneath dried flower 'trees', and concealing florist's foam generally. Although sphagnum and reindeer moss are available commercially, other mosses are useful by-products of long walks, and can serve the same purposes. Not only country or woodland walks – mosses, and the similar liverworts, are great colonizers of bare, windswept places, whether along the sea coast or on high, rocky mountains. Chalky, acid, sandy soils; stream-sides; pastures and meadows; conifer woods, mixed woods, and single-species woods all have their own particular communities of tiny, non-flowering plants. In cities, garden walls and roofs – even cracks in pavements – support certain types of moss. Tree trunks and stumps, especially in damp woodland, are treasure troves of various and luxurious mosses, liverworts and lichens.

Mosses and liverworts are tolerant of shade, but those growing in deciduous woodlands tend to put on most of their new growth in spring, before the leaf canopy is fully developed. (Lichens need more light and usually put on most of their growth in winter, or in sunny, open places.)

Very few mosses have common names, as most have no commercial value. The Linnaean names are of little use to anyone but botanists, as the differences between one genus or species and another are often microscopic. For the flower arranger, it is simply a question of choosing mosses that have a pleasant and suitable appearance.

Some lichens and mosses pull away easily in the hand, or can be peeled easily, from their perch; others need disengaging with a sharp knife. Try to cut away the soil or debris clinging to their roots, while still keeping the moss or lichen intact; tiny, crumbly bits are not worth keeping. Bring a light-weight basket or box and plenty of newspaper with you, so you can place a sheet of newspaper between each layer of moss. This prevents the upper surfaces becoming soiled by the roots of the layer above it. As with harvesting other material, try to collect on a dry day.

Types of Moss

If you want to collect sphagnum moss (*Sphagnum* spp) rather than buy it, look in damp bogs, with nutrient-deficient, acid water, usually in areas of high rainfall. (The decayed remains of sphagnum moss form sphagnum peat, sold in garden centres for soil improvement.) Sphagnum moss produces dense mats of leafy rosettes, and ranges in colour from bright yellow-green to ruddy brown, sometimes tinged with pink or purple. Again, it would be pointless to name species, but compact-growing types are most useful.

Sphagnum collected fresh, or bought fresh from a florist, can be squeezed until as dry as possible, then dried completely outdoors in sun, in a warm airing cupboard, or in a low oven, with the door left open so moisture can escape. (The latter method will put paid to any insects, as well.) Sphagnum sometimes contains bits of twigs or other impurities, which can be teased out if necessary.

The silvery, cushion-like moss *Leucobryum glaucum* is found in damp woodlands and moorlands. Like sphagnum, it is hollow celled and can absorb water, but it dries to an attractive silvery colour, a bit like dense, lacy

Although moss has largely been replaced by florist's foam as foundations for fresh and dried-flower displays, moss can be used as a highly visible decorative feature. Only half a dozen flowers, for example, can transform a shallow dish of moss into a delightful miniature moss garden.

artemisia foliage. It is one of the few mosses threatened with extinction, because it is collected on a large scale for sale, and should be taken with restraint. This, and most other mosses, will dry *in situ* in an arrangement, but if you are worried about its moisture content harming adjacent dried flowers or foliage, air dry it, in a single layer, on absorbent kitchen paper or newspaper. A radiator or night-store heater will accelerate the drying process.

Reindeer moss (*Cladonia rangiferina*), also called tundra moss or Iceland moss, is rather more difficult to find growing in its natural environment, unless you live in arctic or sub-arctic regions. There, this silvery-grey, much-branched plant – technically a lichen – grows abundantly and composes the staple diet of reindeer, but it can sometimes be found in high altitudes with similar conditions, such as mountains in Scotland. Reindeer moss is commercially harvested, dried and sold, either in its natural colour or dyed, and is extremely expensive. However, other, very similar species can be found growing wild in dense cushions or clumps on heathlands, moors and on the edge of bogs; others still grow by the sea, on sand dunes and on shingle. If you do manage to collect a similar lichen, dry as for *Leucobryum*.

Bun moss (*Grimmia pulvinata*) is not often available commercially, but its compact, dome-shaped cushions can be found on roofs and the copings of walls, especially limestone. A similar species grows on rocks near the sea; in cities, the delicate moss *Orthotrichum diaphanum* forms bun-like cushions on fences, walls, cracks in pavings and trees. Dry as above.

There are over 600 species of selaginella, an attractive, fern-like club moss, largely from the tropics and subtropics. One species (*Selaginella selaginoides*) grows in mountains in cool temperate climates, such as in Scotland and northern England. Certain tropical species are sold as pot plants for greenhouses, particularly for edging benches. In the right conditions and given enough humidity, some are rampant growers and can be cut and dried; new growth will quickly appear. Any pot plants of selaginella that fail to thrive can be dried and given a second life in dried flower displays.

Techniques – Cleaning

There is never any question about cleaning fresh flowers, as death overtakes them before dust can settle. Dried flowers, however, with their longer life span, eventually get dusty, and this is one of the main criticisms levelled against them, rather unfairly. Certainly, many have subtle colouring, and a thick layer of dust does nothing to enhance this subtlety.

Avoid permanently displaying dried flowers where dust is liable to accumulate – near windows, for example. (The light from windows is equally unhelpful, causing bright colours to fade.) Open, solid-fuel burning fireplaces can also cover nearby surfaces with dust. Placing dried arrangements in potentially dusty spots for a dinner party or Christmas festivities does no harm, provided you return them to a more suitable place afterwards. But even in the most modern, air-conditioned environment, dust is inevitable.

When an arrangement becomes dusty, gently brush the surfaces of petals, leaves or pods with a fine dry paintbrush or nail varnish brush. Spider webs can also be troublesome; use a brush or other pointed object – a pencil, for example – to ensnare them. Twist it round and round, like building up spun sugar on a cone, to

remove the web, making sure you get all the tiny, thread-like wisps that can hang, like beards, from the material. (Removing a spider web from a teasel head can take several minutes of concentrated effort!)

Wipe dusty glycerined foliage with a damp cloth or cotton wool. Some people use a tiny bit of vegetable oil dabbed onto a dry cloth, to give a lustrous finish to glycerined foliage. Large, broad-leaved subjects, such as aspidistra or fatsia leaves, are particularly suitable. Glycerined material that has been stored for any length of time may also need wiping, to remove bits of debris from other material stored with it, and a bit of oil to renew its sheen.

An alternative approach to dust is to enclose the arrangement in a glass case, either an old-fashioned bell jar or battery jar, or less expensive replica. While the flowers do remain dust-free, it is impractical for large displays and any feeling of informality or intimacy is lost. Then, too, several glass-enclosed displays in one room tend to emphasize the lifelessness of the flowers, like relics displayed in reliquaries in some Italian churches.

If you have done your best, and an arrangement still looks dusty, throw it out; its decorative life is over.

Repairs Although most books on dried flower arranging have large sections on repairs, in practice very little repair work is necessary. If a stem snaps in half, there is nothing shameful in treating the accident as a challenge, and reusing the material in its shortened form. If one or two lower florets fall from a flower spike, set it deep into the arrangement, so the loss is hidden. If a flower snaps at the neck, you can use it, as is, in potpourri or for decorating presents. Decapitated seed pods, such as poppy, mallow and sea holly, can also be used to form the centres of over-fluffy helichrysum; carefully remove any remaining bits of fluff first, then glue the two together.

If you do have your heart set on using a certain flower of a certain height, and the stem snaps, lengthen it, as for naturally stubby material (see pages 72-73). If the stem is hollow, try inserting a wire into both pieces, like a dowel, and rejoin them. For very heavy material, such as cardoon, artichoke and sunflower heads, use a wooden dowel instead of wire. (Use a dab of glue at the join, or bind with florist's tape.)

If a few petals are missing from a flower, and the centre is attractive, remove the other petals and use the centre alone. Rudbeckias, or cone flowers, can be treated in this way; so can chamomile, feverfew and leopard's bane. Again, if you have your heart set on using a particularly exquisite flower, use a dot of quick drying glue, applied with a tooth pick, to re-attach the petals.

You can use also glue preventively, putting a drop of glue at notoriously weak joins, such as where tulip or paeony petals are attached to the flower head, before preserving material in a desiccant. Allow the glue to thoroughly dry first. Bells of Ireland and Chinese lanterns can have each joint between stalk or calyx and stem reinforced with glue, once the material is fully dried or glycerined.

Polyurethene spray can be applied to fluffy material such as clematis, milkweed and rosebay willow herb seed heads, and bulrush and pampas grass, to prevent it disintegrating, but harvesting at the correct time is more important. Hair spray is sometimes used, but its scent is more reminiscent of hairdresser's salons than green fields and gardens.

Dried flower heads such as leeks or roses that have become misshapen can be steamed until pliable, then gently reshaped by hand or, in the case of alliums, shaken out. Hold the head above steam from a kettle for few seconds, being careful not to burn yourself.

Although most damage is a result of handling during the course of preserving or arranging, some may occur while the flowers are on display, and one or two broken flower heads can give an entire arrangement an abandoned look. Just as you inspect fresh displays from time to time, to remove wilted flowers, inspect dried arrangements for signs of wear and tear. It may be the defective material can be removed without further ado. If huge gaps are created, replace with 'fresh' or rearrange, perhaps using a new container or two smaller ones.

Decorating Hats

Wide brimmed straw hats are inexpensive, easy to wear and very easy to customize with dried flowers. Both natural and dyed straw are suitable, the low key of the former making a non-strident setting for natural-coloured flowers. If you want to change the colour scheme of the flowers, to suit different outfits, choose natural or dyed black or white straw. Pastels and strident primary and secondary colours are more limiting, although they can also be stunning.

Dried flowers on a hat are more vulnerable than those on a table or bookcase, but if you treat them with care, they should last for several wearings. With floppy straw hats, keep the dried material tightly round the crown. Rigid straw hats, such as boaters, provide more stable bases, and the brim as well as the crown can be decorated.

If the weave is loose enough, you can insert the stems of wild or cultivated grasses and grains, such as hare's-tail grass, wheat or oat, through the weave, so that the grains rest across the brim. Insert the grass singly or in small clusters, but never force a stem through the weave. If a stem seems loose, tack it in position with toning cotton. Angle the stems slightly, to avoid a spoke-like effect, and if you are using the stems at regular intervals, angle them in the same direction. Long grasses hanging over the rim can look attractive, but are liable to snap off, so be prepared to replace them. Lastly, a few stems of corn or barley worked in amongst a posy or garland or artificial flowers on a pre-decorated hat can improve its looks considerably.

To make a garland of dried flowers to fit round the crown, build it up on a flat ribbon rather than directly on the hat. Use 2.5-3.7cm (1-1½in) grosgrain, allowing extra for a bow and/or trailing streamers, if wished. Although you can tie the decorated ribbon onto the hat, it is neater and less risky to sew it on, adding the bow and streamers separately. Measure the perimeter of the crown at its base, and mark the dimensions on the ribbon, leaving at least 2.5cm (1in) extra on both ends, for attaching.

It is easier to attach small bunches of flowers

Hats are for hanging as well as for wearing. This trio of straw hats sports dried-flower decorations, ranging from a simple cluster of helichrysum and dried grasses, right, to a swag of larkspur and hare's tail grass, built on a foundation of braided raffia, centre, and a mini-arrangement of echinops, blue-dyed hair grass and silver-flowered xeranthemum on a florist's foam base, shown on the extreme right.

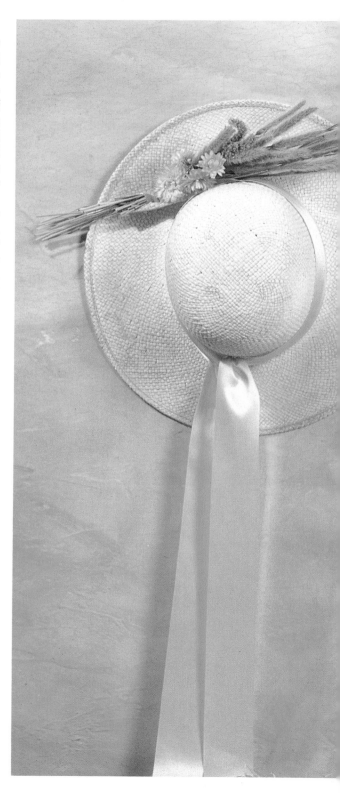

Making a decorated hat band

Wire a small bunch of flowers, seed heads and grasses, such as delphinium, gomphrena, poppy seed heads and decorative grass flower heads.

Cut the wired stems and bind with florist's tape. Prepare as many bunches as necessary to create the desired effect on the grosgrain ribbon, already measured to fit around the crown of the hat.

Sew the bunches onto the grosgrain, beginning at the centre. Overlap them to hide the taped stems, until the garland is complete and ready to attach to the hat.

than individual ones. Use silver reel wire to make bunches of single types of flower or combinations, such as roses, helipterum and gypsophila; or delphinium florets, cornflowers and lady's mantle. (You might want to work in a few feather flowers or simple clusters of feathers.) Cut the wired stems to leave 1-2cm (½-¾in), then bind with florist's tape. Sew the taped stems to the ribbon, trying to keep flowers that extend beyond the ribbon along the top edge only, to avoid crushing them against the brim.

Work from the centre towards the ends – you can make the central bunch slightly larger, as a focal point – or from one end to the other. If you want a bow, leave a good-sized gap of plain ribbon at both ends, to avoid visual confusion where dried flowers and bow meet. Overlap the bunches as you proceed, to hide the stems and because the flowers spread out slightly when the ribbon is wrapped round the hat. Make one or two extra bunches, to cover the join, if necessary, or replace later damages.

Once the correct length of ribbon is covered with flowers, but with the ends exposed, sew it to the hat, front and back. Make sure any central feature is truly central, and tuck the ends of the ribbon under to fit. Sew on the bow and streamers, if using; or if ribbon is exposed at the join, attach one of the reserve bunches.

For a more casual decoration, use a narrow braid of raffia instead of a ribbon, and widely space the attached bunches of flowers, so the raffia shows.

A single, larger posy of dried flowers, at the front, side or back of the hat can be equally attractive, and takes less time. Make one side flat, to fit against the brim or crown, as wished, and build it up in the position from which it will be viewed.

Making Unusual Containers

Although the idea of decorative vases based on tin cans and empty jars recalls the messy but heart-warming projects brought home from nursery school, sophisticated containers can also be made of modest components. By covering a container with dried or glycerined flowers, foliage or pods, the container and its contents can 'read' as a single object; a jar covered with overlapping sprigs of glycerined beech leaves, for example, would merge into an arrangement of glycerined beech branches and dried flowers. Light-hearted visual jokes can also be made; a tin covered with tightly packed helichrysum heads could contain a display of dried foliage alone; or an informal, hay-wrapped tin could contain dozens of formal, long-stemmed dried roses.

Natural Camouflage Camouflaging tins and jars with dried material is an excellent way of using up odds and ends of stemless flower heads and seed pods: a ring of poppy heads glued round the neck of a sphagnum moss-covered jar, for example, or tiny delphinium or larkspur buds randomly embedded into a moss covering, to create a meadow-like effect.

As well as glycerined foliage, hay and sphagnum moss, other plant possibilities include dried reindeer moss, bun moss, potpourri, raffia, corn husks, woven grass matting, oriental rush wall coverings and split bamboo place mats. Chamois leather, suede off-cuts and natural linen, either stretched tight or loosely wrapped; overlapping feathers, and pieces of bark can conceal a jar or tin, and make direct references to nature. Biscuit tins, roasting tins, wooden vegetable or fruit boxes, plastic dustbins or even sturdy cardboard boxes can be camouflaged for large-scale displays.

Use quick-drying glue, applied and left until slightly tacky, or florist's, or ordinary mastic, put on in strips parallel to the top and bottom of the container. Large containers may need additional mastic strips in the middle. (For lightweight fabric-type coverings, double-sided tape or mastic may do the trick more effectively than glue.) If you are using glue and the container is large, you may have to do one side or area at a time. You can sometimes simply tie camouflage into position, with strands of raffia, ribbons or even rubber bands; it depends on your standards of perfection and the permanence of the display.

Fabric To apply fabric-like coverings (suede and woven grass matting, for example) as a single, close-fitting piece, use a straight-sided container. Turn it on its side on one corner of the fabric, then mark the width of the container. Use a piece of string or measuring tape to mark its circumference, or overall length, if it is rectangular. Cut the covering to the length and width needed. Allow for an overlap where the two ends of fabric meet, and extra for any 'collar' along the top rim. Apply the glue or strips of mastic to the container, fix the covering firmly to the container, turning over and glueing any overlapping edge to make a tidy finish. Trim any excess as necessary and finish with two or three parallel bands of raffia or ribbon, tied with attractive bows.

Easier still is to place a small container in the centre of a square of fabric, such as a linen or cotton handkerchief or silk scarf, large enough for all edges to slightly overlap the rim. Pull the centre of each of the four sides up to the rim of the container, so the corners fold evenly outwards, then secure just under the rim with a rubber band, raffia or ribbon. Arrange the overhang into a decorative ruff. Or draw up the fabric into four points, as above, then tightly secure the overhanging fabric in two side bunches (rather like rabbit ears), using short lengths of stub wire to secure them. Side-bunching is particularly suitable for globe-shaped containers.

Foliage Large, perfect specimens of glycerined laurel, rhododendron or magnolia can be arranged vertically and slightly overlapping, with their points above the rim of the container, like soldiers on parade. Smaller leaves can overlap one another in a less formal way, for a tapestry-like effect, and mixed as well as single types could be used. (When building up a covering of foliage, do not worry about it overhanging the bottom rim; it can be snipped off once the container is completely covered.) Moss, straw and hay are messy, and for a smooth, evenly dense surface, it is usually necessary to patch several pieces or sections together, and trim the finished covering along the top and bottom rim.

Gourds Sophisticated-looking containers can be made from ornamental hard-shelled gourds, of the genus *Lagenaria*. Variously called white-flowered gourds, bottle gourds, calabash gourds and turk's turban, they can be round, oval, bottle-shaped or club shaped. Cut when fully ripe, and the skins feel hard when rapped. Leave 2.5cm (1in) of stalk attached. Although they feel hard, they can be easily bruised at this stage, so do not drop or stack them. Dry them, not touching one another, on a cake rack or raised wire mesh screen, in a warm, airy place, for several months. Turn them over from time to time; a small proportion inevitably go mouldy, but you can wipe surface mould off with a damp cloth. When fully dry, rest the gourd on a flat surface to see how it 'sits'; long gourds are sometimes better used horizontally than vertically. (Gourds with hopelessly uneven bottoms can be displayed on little, purpose-built tripods of bamboo or wooden dowels, tied in the middle with twine or raffia.) Draw the outline of a hole on the top, then cut the hole, using a sharp knife or a small saw, if necessary. Scrape away the insides, and file smooth the cut edge, if wished. A similar treatment can be given to coconut shells, sawn across the top and hollowed out.

Stem Sections Sections of thick hollow stems, such as bamboo, angelica or giant hogweed can be used as containers, but may need weighting down with an inner core of quick-drying plaster for stability. On a larger scale, hollow sections or chunks of wood, such as arbutus, birch, ornamental-barked maple and cherry can be cleaned up, sawn level and polished or left as is. They make ideal containers for miniature gardens. It is easier to enlarge an existing hole than to hollow out a solid section of wood, which involves drilling closely spaced holes around the desired diameter, then drilling over the entire surface and chiselling the wood out. A shallow stockade of thick branches, of roughly the same height and diameter, can be inter-woven with bands of raffia or twine, then glued or nailed to a chipboard base.

Making Garlands

The words 'garland', 'wreath', and 'swag' are used interchangeably in many books on flower arranging. The words are sometimes given as synonyms for each other in dictionaries, adding to the confusion. Here, however, a garland is defined as a flexible, elongated construction of flowers and foliage, decoratively hung, draped or rested. Garlands are traditionally used to encircle columns and tables at weddings or other festive celebrations. They can also be entwined spirally down columns and staircase handrails, and used as focal points on walls – above a mantelpiece or mirror, or over an arched doorway, for example. A garland could also be placed down the middle of a dining-table, or hung from a pair of tall table candel-abras, as a spectacular centrepiece.

As with swags and wreaths (see page 74) the appearance should be one of abundance. In addition, garlands should be visually strong enough to make an impression from some distance away; consider a garland as part of the architecture of a room, in spite of the delicacy of its components. Much more material is needed to make a luxurious garland than a swag or wreath, however, and if material is limited, the foundation – ribbons, upholstery cord, hay, moss or plaited raffia, for example – can become part of the design. Realistic-looking artificial conifer 'ropes' make good foundations, especially for Christmas decora-tions – they are available more widely in America than in England. All of these reduce the amount of time and dried material needed to construct the display.

You can also achieve an appearance of abundance by using a large proportion of fresh, long-lasting evergreen foliage, such as elaeag-nus, ivy, or Portugal laurel, with a relatively small amount of dried flowers. This approach can be time consuming and the display lasts only as long as the foliage.

Decide on the shape of the garland. It can be a single, large loop; a series of loops of equal depth; or a large central loop, surrounded by loops of diminishing depth. A garland can be stretched tightly around the rim of a table or hung on a wall. An illusion of central depth can be created by making the garland generously full, but larger in the middle, and tapering symmetrically towards the edges. Looped gar-lands against walls can also have hanging drops at each end.

Decide, too, whether the flowers are to be evenly distributed along the length of the garland; clustered into focal points; or a single, central display. With a modest amount of dried material, clusters tend to be more effective than even distribution.

Method Measure the length of garland needed, allowing a bit extra for overlap, if it is to fit round a table. You can use foundation ribbons, cords, wires or ropes, or a piece of string if it is more convenient. Mark the number and positions of any loops. Mark the centre of a single loop, if you want a graduated thickness or a central focal point. Lay the measured material out on the floor or work surface, and place the dried material along its length, approximately as it is to be used. This gives an idea of the density and prevents a lop-sided display. (Put some dried material on one side for repairs or filling any bald spots that may appear when the garland is hung.)

A garland can be built up in various ways. The simplest is using lengths of ribbons, upholstery cord or plaited raffia to form the loops, with a central cluster of flowers or smaller clusters placed at every point formed by two loops. Many tiny bunches of dried material, with or without fresh foliage, can be overlapped to form a continuous decorative rope, bound together with reel wire onto a core of wire, clothes-line or cord. If you are making a garland of heavy material, such as pine cones, acorns, nuts and seed pods, use clothes-line or a thick cord.

Lengths of stub wire can be formed into circles, covered with moss, hay or raffia bound with strands of raffia, then decorated with dried flowers and formed into chain links. One traditional method for making large-scale dried flower garlands is to cut long strips of 2.5cm (1in) wire mesh netting, about 20cm (8in) wide, then wrap and wire them closed round a central core of dried sphagnum moss. The mesh is flattened on one side, so the tubes hang neatly, then decorated. For very long garlands, several tubes can be linked together, end to end. Whatever the foundation, remember that the finished garland is seen from above and below as well as straight on; as with wreaths and swags, the dried material should wrap round accordingly, with only the back flat.

Making swags and garlands

Using silver reel wire, make small, tight bunches of flowers. You can make mixed bunches, as shown, or bunches of single species. Make more bunches than you think you need, as inevitably gaps appear once the swag or garland is hung, and infill material comes in handy.

Form the end of medium-gauge reel wire into a loop for hanging, then begin wiring overlapping bunches of flowers along the wire, using silver reel wire to fix. Continue until the desired length is reached, then cut the medium-gauge wire, allowing a little extra for hanging, if necessary.

For a thicker, more rigid swag, wrap chicken wire around a central core of sphagnum moss, and bend to shape. Attach preformed bunches of flowers to the foundation, overlapping them, as above.

Styles of Arrangement

Like many other religious festivals, Easter can be celebrated on two levels. It is a serious religious occasion, marking the Resurrection of Christ and, in another sense, the re-birth of spring. Secondly, Easter is a jovial and highly commercialized seasonal event, for children and adults alike. Traditional Easter egg hunts on the lawn, and, in America, Easter parades and Easter hats, mark the occasion.

Arrangements for Easter

White, symbolizing purity, is the traditional floral colour for Easter; yellow, the colour of seasonal daffodils and primroses, has also come to be associated with Easter. Dried material offers a wealth of yellows: yellow roses, various helichrysums, craspedia, achillea, mimosa, Jerusalem sage, statice, goldenrod and alchemilla, to name a few. Much of the dried material thought of as white, however, is actually creamy white, or with overtones of grey, blue, green or brown. Nonetheless, honesty seed pods, gypsophila, white statice, helipterums, ammobium, white delphinium and branches of cotton (*Gossypium herbaceum*) pods are reasonably white. In addition, some commercial growers offer bleached material, including quaking grass, hare's tail grass, broom bloom and achillea, which approximate white; these may have to be ordered specially.

The crown-of-thorns imagery can be translated into a floral display with leafless branches of hawthorn, sea buckthorn, manzanita, or the exquisitely green but fiercely spiny *Poncirus trifoliata*, or even arching branches of wild blackberry. A circular woven ring of such branches could be filled with low, tightly packed dried flowers in whites and yellows. A simple, vertical arrangement, perhaps with dried flowers clustering at the base of tall branches, or tall spikes of white delphinium rising from a base of thorny twigs, would convey a feeling of ascendency in a subtle way.

Easter is as much a children's festivity as it is a serious religious occasion, and Easter baskets and Easter eggs are among the most popular decorations. Helichrysum, anaphalis, hare's tail grass, yarrow, sunray and cluster-flowered everlasting, in shades of yellow and white, form a decorative rim and handle. White duck eggs, as shown, or smaller white hen's eggs, can be displayed in their natural colour, or dipped in vegetable dye to match.

There is a case to be made for combining dried flowers and fresh green foliage at Easter. Not only does the green serve as contrast to the yellows and whites, but it contributes an element of vitality which dried flowers, however beautiful, lack. Use a large, decorative outer container with an inner jar; either surround a central display of dried flowers with a dense ring of fresh foliage kept fresh in water, or vice versa.

Eggs On the lighter side are all the possible variations on the Easter egg and nest theme. A nest can be woven of raffia or pliable twigs, such as pussy willow or hazel, then lined with moss; or made of sphagnum moss glued to the inside and outside of plastic food tubs or round aluminium freezer containers. Sprigs of short-stemmed flowers can be interwoven, and stemless flower heads glued directly onto moss. Dyed hard-boiled eggs can fill a large nest, or miniature, foil-wrapped eggs fill a small one. For a naturalistic touch, a few feathers could be rested in the nest, see page 50. Attractive artificial, but feathered, birds can be had inexpensively from many oriental stores; perch one on the edge of a suitably-sized nest, for a finishing touch.

Young children, particularly, enjoy immediate possession and instant gratification. Therefore small, chocolate egg-filled nests made of moss glued to chopped-off yoghurt cartons make excellent individual place setting decorations for a children's party. (Putting the name of each guest on a nest will prevent possible mix-ups, when it is time to take the nests home.)

Easter Bonnets

For an American Easter table centrepiece, an inexpensive straw hat can be rested right-way up, then decorated with masses of dried flowers, in pastel pinks and blues as well as the traditional yellow and white. As it is a temporary display, the flowers can be rested or sewn rather than laboriously wired on. Toning ribbon streamers can be arranged to trail attractively along the table. A long dining-table could have several such hats; individual place settings could be dolls' straw hats in toning colours, each containing a tiny posy.

Victorian Arrangements

The Victorian era spanned sixty-four years, and inevitably attitudes to flower arranging developed and changed during that time. There were also minor schools of thought which advocated different, often more advanced, styles from those popular at the time. However, elaborate ornamentation is the hallmark of mid- and late Victorian style, whether furniture design, architecture, garden design or flower arranging. For some time afterwards, 'Victorian' became the password for overly ornate, and to describe something as Victorian was automatically pejorative. Many Victorian works of art, architecture, domestic objects and so on, that had intrinsic merit were condemned, together with the genuinely dreadful excesses of the time.

The best of Victorian style is currently enjoying renewed popularity, although the Victorian passion for drawing moral conclusions from the botanical structures of flowers, or of using individual flowers to convey specific sentiments, is gone. The Victorian posy, usually a central rose bud surrounded by concentric rings of flowers and finished with a lacy frill, (see page 149) is now fashionable for weddings. Densely packed masses of mixed flowers in ornate containers, typical of Victorian flower arrangements, are also popular, in a toned-down form.

Colour Several theories of combining colours were in vogue in Victorian times. These included using some pastel colours, but primarily using intensely rich and contrasting colours. The Victorians enjoyed deriving guidance from nature; they saw the yellows and purples of pansies, for example, or the red and green of woody nightshade berries, as a divine lesson in colour co-ordination, to be followed when arranging cut flowers. Their flower arrangements were like miniature versions of their violently hued bedding schemes. All-white arrangements were also popular, as white symbolized purity, another concept held in high esteem.

Towards the end of the Victorian era, there was an enlightened movement towards a simpler approach. Limiting the number of different colours and types of flowers in a single

A glorious medley of Victoriana, fresh roses and dried flowers, left, makes a charmingly nostalgic display.

display was advocated, and was harmony, not contrast, and spaciousness, not crowding.

The Victorians were great collectors, and any exotic flower, newly introduced from abroad, enjoyed immediate popularity, as did those, such as dahlias, that could be hybridized. (The Victorians were as scientific as they were sentimental.) They enthused over beautiful flowers, such as roses; and grotesque flowers, such as strelitzia and cockscomb, in equal measure. Eclecticism is the key.

One excellent cue that the Victorians took from nature was the use of foliage to complement the colour of cut flowers; ivy and ferns were particularly popular, and leaves of tropical foliage plants, such as begonia and *Cissus antarctica*, were also used. In a suprisingly modern way, the Victorians included wild flowers, seed heads and foliage with cultivated ones.

Containers The containers, as much as the flowers, identify a display as Victorian. Containers were often as elaborate as the flowers they contained. Hand-painted or enamelled, gilded, porcelain, such as Sèvres and Limoges, was favoured. Sometimes these were further decorated with three-dimensional porcelain roses,

carnations or zinnias. Glass, in various forms, was another favourite: cut glass, milk glass, cranberry glass, shaded satin glass, clear and ruby-red Bohemian glass, Bristol glass and Venetian glass. Parian, a type of porcelain that resembles marble, allowed the newly wealthy middle classes to purchase inexpensive 'marble' statues, busts and vases, some heavily encrusted with tiny, three-dimensional bunches of grapes, vine leaves and tendrils.

Certain shapes were popular: a hand-shaped vase, handled vases and moulded jugs. The multi-layered epergne, used to decorate the centre of dining-tables, was often filled with a lavish display of fruit, moss and flowers. Towards the end of the era, though, visionaries such as William Morris and William Robinson were advocating simple containers, such as ginger jars or kitchenware, to echo the simplicity of the flowers.

Equally Victorian is the glass dome, used to keep dust off wax, shell or feather flowers; stuffed birds, or other delicate displays. Such a dome is ideal for covering flowers which have been dried in silica gel, as they are particularly sensitive to atmospheric moisture.

Glass bell jars, above, were used by Victorians to protect dried flower and other displays from dust. Genuine Victorian bell jars are expensive, but reasonably priced reproductions are available. Bell jars are particularly useful for protecting flowers preserved in desiccant from atmospheric moisture.

Indoor Dried Gardens

Although summer in a garden is lovely, spring is probably the season when people without gardens miss them most. The lively challenge of getting a garden back into shape, shopping sprees at garden centres, and observing in detail the progress of emerging bulbs and newly awakening trees and shrubs, elude the gardenless.

Indoor minature gardens can offer solace and pleasure, to those with gardens as well as those without. The serious gardener can attempt to mimic nature in miniature with terrariums or Wardian cases, and pre-mixed but short-lived planting in decorative bowls is another alternative. Indoor gardens of dried material are rarely available commercially, but are easy to make and never die. You can rearrange them from time to time, and replace the flowers with new ones for the changing seasons or at whim.

Shallow containers are usually best: the large terra cotta saucers that are sold for placing under terra cotta pots are ideal, as they reinforce the imagery of living plants. Old-fashioned terra cotta half pans, used for growing cacti and alpines, are an alternative. Shallow wicker baskets, fluted-edged porcelain dishes, carving boards and wooden bread boards, are alternatives. Plastic or aluminium foil containers are sometimes recommended, but they detract from the finished effect. If you use a glass container, line the sides with moss, as well as the top.

The 'lawn', as in real gardens, is an important feature and should be positioned first. Tightly packed bun moss (Grimmia) makes a velvety, if slightly lumpy, sward. Sphagnum moss is less bumpy and more carpet-like, although its surface is rougher and more open, and you may have to do some judicious cobbling or trimming with manicure scissors, to get it into shape. You can use either fresh moss, and it will dry in situ, or dried. Very shallow baskets can simply be packed with moss, although it is then difficult to support tall dried flowers or twigs in the moss alone. Most containers should have a layer of florist's foam, onto which the moss is fixed with hairpins or bent wires. For rimless bases, either impale large sections of moss directly onto florist's frogs, held in place with mastic; or build a shallow foundation of florist's foam, as above.

Although traditional lawn fanatics spend much time and effort eradicating lawn daisies, some dried helipterums or ammobiums tucked into the moss would give a pleasantly life-like touch. Remember that you are designing a landscape; flowers that are clustered together are usually more effective than those that are randomly distributed. If your garden is to be viewed from above, check it from that position as you build up the display; likewise, if it is to be viewed from all directions or only from one direction, plan accordingly.

Consistency in scale is important. Carefully selected and pruned twigs or stems, such as those of hazel or gypsophila, become trees; sprigs of glycerined box become hedging, clipped into shape with manicure scissors. Selected water-washed pebbles become boulders in a landscape, and a piece of lichen-covered fruit-tree bark becomes a massive fallen tree trunk.

A dried garden can be made in a cylindrical glass container or Wardian case, although the atmosphere inside must be bone dry, rather than moist. Build a little mossy knoll, using gently shaped pieces of florist's foam for a foundation, perhaps with a contorted willow or hazel 'tree' on top.

An old-fashioned wooden cutlery tray could become the base for a formal garden, with rows of different coloured flowers growing neatly from each section.

The man-made paraphernalia of gardens can be repeated in miniature. Little winding paths, tiny dolls' garden furniture, mirrors to represent water, arbours supporting tiny dried roses; statuary, and even gnomes, are possible, according to taste.

Lastly, indoor dried gardens need not be miniature. A room divider, normally filled with house plants, could be filled instead with moss and tall spikes of delphinium, eucalyptus, hazel or alder branches, or for a life-size dried garden, birch or hazel trees sawn off at ground level and set in quick-drying plaster.

Masses of fresh moss and a pair of oriental ivory birds form the basis of this indoor dried garden. A cluster of dried timothy grass and polygonum gives a sense of scale, and the lawn daisies are tiny helipterums. The moss will dry as it ages, retaining much of its fresh green colour.

117

Miniatures

In the world of flower arranging competitions, miniatures must be under 10cm (4in) high; floral displays between 10-23cm (4-9in) high fall into the 'petite' category. Entries can be disqualified for exceeding the maximum dimension by a fraction of an inch, but for the ordinary flower arranger, the particular dimensions are less important than the over-all effect. A tiny flower arrangement should make the viewer marvel at its scaled-down delicacy, balance and perfection and, like Alice in *Through the Looking Glass*, experience a fleeting view of a world in miniature.

The three, equally important components of miniature displays are the dried flowers, the container and the setting. More than any other type of dried flower display, miniatures must be placed where they are safe from accidental damage and can be seen without the distractions of ordinary household clobber. Miniatures can sometimes be more impressive when displayed in multiples or clusters, perhaps in a glass case or an old-fashioned wooden printer's tray, hung on a wall. A large perspex tray on a low coffee table could hold a dozen miniatures, variations on a single colour theme or using twelve different displays in identical containers. Dressing tables or bedside tables are potentially suitable, provided that they are not already crowded.

Containers These can vary from exquisite Victorian silver, ivory or bone miniature boxes to plastic bottle or toothpaste lids, although the latter rarely look like anything other than plastic lids, however hard people try. Natural containers or bases include small seashells, tiny pieces of driftwood, slate, granite stones and minerals. Halved walnut shells make good containers, tough, inexpensive and ideal for children to work with. Toy shops and oriental shops may have dolls' china tea sets, attractive enough to fill with dried flowers. (Antique miniature china samples, carried by travelling salesmen to display their wares, are also suitable, but rare and very expensive.) As with ordinary-sized containers, not all miniature containers are inherently attractive. Crested Victorian miniature china, for example, may be very collectable, but some examples are oddly proportioned.

Empty perfume flasks, miniature liqueur flasks, and glass cosmetic jars, such as those for eye shadow, are often attractive enough to reuse in miniature dried flower displays. With narrow necked miniature containers, either wedge a small piece of florist's foam onto the neck, or build up a small mound of mastic, into which flower stems are pushed. Pill boxes and snuff boxes can be opened and filled with small pieces of florist's foam, cut to fit.

Some dried material is naturally miniature: glixia, for example, crocosmia seed heads, quaking grass and gypsophila. Others, such as achillea, hydrangea, delphinium and larkspur can be taken apart into florets. Perennial sea lavender (*Limonium latifolium*) is much more delicate than the annual statice (*L. sinuatum*) and a single stem can provide a dozen little branchlets covered with tiny white or pale-mauve flowers. Likewise, a single fern frond can provide many frondlets from both sides of its midrib. You may have to wire up some material, such as delphinium and hydrangea florets, gypsophila sprigs and single ivy leaves, as their own stems are weak or non-existent. Use short lengths of silver reel wire. However, there are many dried flowers with stalks or stems stiff enough not to need support.

The kitchen can be a source of miniature containers as well as bodily sustenance: egg cups; tiny mortars; silver tea strainers and salt cellars; porcelain dariole moulds, ramekins and butter warmers; and tinned steel tartlet tins and patty tins. Lastly, old-fashioned porcelain pie funnels can double up as miniature containers, and a porcelain blackbird, the most traditional of all, can carry a tiny posy in its beak.

A miniature, dried flower bonsai takes about two hours to make. This little bonsai has an oak branchlet as the foundation, which is florist's foam disguised with dried reindeer moss and pebbles. Green-dyed broom bloom is its foliage.

119

SUMMER

Summer, even more than spring, provides a wealth of fresh flowers, in the garden, in the wild and in the shops. Enjoying such bounty, even if simply observing distant poppy fields or the beauty of a park or garden, is an inherent part of summer. It is easy to fill the house, for these few months, with almost a surfeit of fresh flowers and forget about future needs. On the other hand, any book on dried flowers that counsels preserving every bloom, at the expense of colour in the garden and fresh colour in the house, is taking a very narrow, dour view indeed. A comfortable compromise can be made, with one eye on the present and another on the winter months ahead.

Mid-and late summer is the prime time for preserving foliage in glycerine or antifreeze. It is a quick, easy task but an important one, since preserved beech, chestnut, birch and maple leaves, as well as the dozens of suitable garden evergreens, can add bulk and character to even the most modest bunch of store-bought dried flowers. In terms of harvesting flowers and seed pods for drying, the transition from summer to autumn is a subtle one, and many flowers, given a good, hot summer, will be ready for picking and drying or otherwise preserving at this time.

In the Shops

The criteria for buying fresh flowers for drying are no different from those for buying flowers generally. You want blemish-free flowers picked before fully open, but with colour showing in the buds. The flowers should have been picked as recently as possible, and well conditioned. Material to be preserved in desiccants, especially silica gel, is the most liable to fail due to lack of freshness. For this method, any shop-bought flowers are risky, because even those newly arrived at the shop may have spent several days in transit from the grower.

You can sometimes walk into a florist's, and get an immediate sense of decay: the floor might be unswept, the odour of algae-filled water drifts through the air, flower display containers are empty, and the attendant is nowhere to be seen. Inspecting the flowers is pointless, and a tactful, polite retreat is sensible. Other florist's shops appear spotlessly clean, well attended with fresh-looking stock; these are far more likely to be successful.

Most florists go to wholesale suppliers on the same days every week: early Monday and Thursday mornings, for example. Try to time your purchases to coincide with the arrival of fresh flowers. If you explain that you want flowers for drying, and that they must be as fresh as possible, reputable florists will oblige. Flowers that have been in cold store for any length of time are usually too charged with water to dry easily.

Ensuring Freshness There are signs you can look out for, which indicate the age and stage of maturity of particular flowers. Soft, rotting or slimy stems and foliage mean that the flowers have been in water for some time. Some flowers change colour as they mature. Cornflowers, for example, change from deep blue to a washed-out blue grey. Many pale or white flowers tend to develop a brown edging to the petals or take on a papery, transparent look as they age.

Flowers that grow several to a stem – Peruvian lilies, lilies and delphiniums, for example – usually open and fade from the bottom upwards, so inspect the lower flowers and take note of any flowerless stalks which indicate the removal of faded blooms. The uppermost flowers should still be in bud.

With daisy-like flowers, you can check the centre for the pollen. If the centre is tightly packed like dense pile carpet and, generally, pale, the flower is not yet mature. Once it is fluffy, with yellow powdery pollen visible, it is usually too mature to dry. Sometimes flowers at this stage bulge in the centre, whereas younger blossoms are flat centred. If you study the flowers on a single stem, or those in a bunch, you can often observe the different stages of maturity. Bunches of helichrysum are often sold fresh, for drying. The flowers should just be starting to open, as they continue opening while drying. If the yellow centre is fully visible, they become over-ripe as they dry.

Faded petals on the outside rim of dahlias and similar flowers are other obvious signs of age. Gently and discreetly shaking a bunch of flowers may dislodge old petals that would come off shortly in any case, and reveal what you have to work with.

All this having been said, there are occasional and economical exceptions to the rules. Gypsophila and lady's mantle past their best can be hung upside down to dry, any soggy lower stems having been removed first, and they are usually very successful. This is also true of oldish long-stemmed rose buds, provided they have not started to open. Even delphiniums, which are admittedly dramatic dried as complete spikes, can be dried as smaller sprigs, and you can discard the lower, overmature ones.

Lastly, there are many exotic species of flower which can be bought for fresh display, then dried. These include proteas, banksias, dryandras, mimosa, leucodendrons and silver strawberry (*Leptospermum* spp). Eucalyptus and broom, too, can perform a double duty, first in a fresh arrangement, later as part of a dry one. Galax, with its shiny, round evergreen leaves and wiry stems, is another useful florist's foliage that can be preserved with glycerine, which turns it an attractive pale beige. It is more common in North America than in Britain.

Lack of a garden may limit the range of flowers you can dry or preserve yourself, but shops and market stalls still provide dozens of possibilities. Use the same criteria for buying fresh flowers for drying as you would when buying fresh flowers for immediate arrangement.

In the Garden

Seedlings of annuals sown in drills or broadcast on the open ground may need thinning now. Do this as soon as they are about 2.5cm (1in) high. Using your thumb and forefinger, tease out overcrowded ones, leaving the strongest seedling wherever possible. Spacings do not have to be exact, and can be a bit closer than recommended on the seed packets. The longer thinning is delayed, the more the roots become entangled and the more liable the remaining plants are to suffer damage. Treat those sown in nursery beds to be transplanted as for transplanting half-hardy annuals (see pages 98-99). If the soil is dry, water thoroughly after thinning or transplanting. In very dry weather, sparrows taking dust baths can be troublesome, in which case criss-cross cotton over the beds to give some protection.

Watch out for weeds; the conditions you create in your garden are as ideal for weeds as they are for cultivated plants. Some seed packets have drawings of the particular seedlings, to help you distinguish them. Re-firm and water in, if necessary, any young plants lifted in the course of pulling out weeds. Continue to water whenever the soil is dry.

Perennials, such as tall-growing delphiniums, lupins and paeonies, may need staking, the sooner the better and the less obvious the better. Twiggy pea sticks or hazel sticks are the traditional support, but you can use proprietary metal rings or plastic mesh stretched horizontally above the ground.

Trees and shrubs should be self-maintaining, unless they are newly planted. Keep these, and newly-planted perennials, well watered and free of competition.

Some plants treated as biennials make good dried flower material – sweet William, foxgloves, hollyhocks, mulleins – and early summer is the time to sow them. The method is the same as for sowing annuals (see page 96), although it is more sensible, in view of their long growing time, to raise seedlings in nursery beds, then transplant them into their final position in early autumn. The timing is important; you want tough, compact plants, able to survive the rigours of winter.

Towards midsummer, it is worth visiting garden centres and nurseries, which often have clear-outs of bedding plants then. Traditional gardening books advise against buying such plants, as they are liable to be starved, with yellow leaves, entangled roots and little prospects of producing more flower buds. Although some definitely are beyond the pale, others are just reaching their prime and can be bought for drying or preserving in desiccant. Huge, fat African marigolds, annual dahlias, Prince of Wales's feathers and cockscombs. (The smaller, daintier French marigolds do not dry as well, although they can be preserved in desiccant.)

Harvesting details are given under autumn (see pages 31-33), but some annuals, such as helichrysum, helipterum and cornflowers flower over a long period, starting in midsummer. As you pick them, you encourage the plant to produce more buds. Try, when picking, to leave the buds lower down intact, unless this makes the stem too short. Secondary and later summer flowers may be smaller than the first blooms, but they are still useful.

Lastly, some hardy annuals can be sown towards the end of summer or beginning of autumn – this is the natural timing of self-sown annuals – to flower slightly earlier next summer, or even late spring. Cornflower, larkspur, love-in-a-mist, calendula, alyssum, Shirley poppies and annual scabious are worth trying. Thin, if necessary, before the onset of winter.

Delphiniums, far right, are suitable subjects for drying in a desiccant, such as silica gel or borax. Fortunately, tall spikes of dried larkspur, an annual delphinium, are available commercially, in pink and white as well as shades of blue.
A perennial border, right, in high summer offers a wealth of material for drying. Try to harvest with a modicum of restraint, so the garden retains the bulk of its colour.

When harvesting delicate grasses for drying, handle the material carefully and do not over-fill the basket to minimize damage.

In the Wild

Plants that are regarded as weeds can be usually picked with impunity but some rare or endangered plants are protected by law. Illustrated field guides and local libraries should be able to supply you with the information you need. Theoretically, the land owner's permission must always be obtained before collecting, but in the case of roadsides, hedgerows, fields and woods in the country, and of vacant plots or car parks in the city, it is not always possible. Common sense is usually the best guide.

On the whole, open, sunny places or lightly shaded ones, such as the edge of a woodland, are more productive hunting grounds for flowers and grasses than deep shade, which is better for searching out moss and fungi. For your own comfort and protection during rural expeditions, wear stout gardening gloves. Bring secateurs with you, and a big basket or plastic bag for collection. However lovely the weather, if you are exploring somewhere overgrown, trousers, long sleeves and stout leather shoes or rubber boots are sensible precautions against thorns, insects and other unwelcome creatures, and prickles.

Wild Flowers

The range of wild flowers depends on local conditions, but in northern temperate climates there are some families which are generally widespread. The *Compositae* family is particulary rich, offering cornflowers (*Centaurea cyanus*), various thistles and knapweeds (*Centaurea, Cirsium, Carduus* spp), and the carline thistle (*Carlina vulgaris*). Daisy-like *Compositae* wild flowers include chamomile (*Anthemis nobile*), ox-eye daisy (*Leucanthemum vulgare*), mayweed (*Matricaria recutitia*); yarrow (*Achillea millefolium*), sneezewort (*Achillea ptarmica*) and feverfew (*Chrysanthemum parthenium*). Many of these flowers can also be picked later in the season, as seed heads.

Wild mugwort (*Artemisia vulgaris*) is an unexpected *Compositae*, a modest relative of the many sophisticated *Artemisia* species that fill grey and silver gardens. By the sea, wormwood (*A. absinthum*) and sea wormwood (*A. maritima*) can sometimes be found. For the flower arranger, the tiny flowers of *Artemisia* species are secondary to the mass of silvery foliage, and its aroma – half pungent, half bitter – is said to keep insects away. Wild hop flowers (*Humulus lupulus*) are tiny, but the lantern-like bracts that contain the flowers and the graceful, slender stems from which they hang, are particularly valuable for contrasting with the poker-straight stems of most dried flowers and seed heads.

The white- or pink-flowered bistorts, knotweeds and redshanks all belong to the *Polygonaceae* family, and can be collected in flower or later, in seed. Collect clovers (*Trifolium* spp), which range from the huge red clover (T. *prataense*), to the graceful and small-scale hare's foot clover (T. *arvense*). These can be picked when the flowers are still green, or when they mature and take on shades of silvery pink or purple.

Many wild flowers are classified as garden escapes, not native originally, but capable of surviving and reproducing on their own. Waste ground, especially the sites of long-gone houses or cottages, can sometimes offer good pickings, literally. The yellow-flowered chamomile (*Anthemis tinctora*), leopard's bane (*Doronicum pardalianches*), the fiercely spiny cotton thistle (*Onopordon acanthium*) and some mints, including Corsican mint (*Mentha requienii*) and the silver-leaved horse mint (M. *longifolia*) are garden escapes, suitable for drying. Lastly, some plants, such as goldenrod, are unloved weeds in some northern-temperate countries and carefully cultivated plants in others. Whether found wild or lovingly nurtured, these are worth picking and drying.

Grasses

There is a division in most people's minds between flowers and 'other plants', and grasses, members of *Gramineae*, are placed firmly into the latter category. In fact, they are flowering plants, though the real interest, from the flower arrangers' and agricultural point of view is the seed head. Grasses are particularly useful because many have a lacy delicacy which can soften solid effect of such typical dried material as yarrow or hydrangea. Grasses act

Foxgloves are a prime example of wild plants that have 'crossed the line' and appear, as garden cultivars, in a range of colours and heights. Although modern strains produce larger flowers, more densely packed on the stem, many people prefer the graceful, more delicate appearance of the wild species.

like fine, definitive lines in a rough sketch. Being virtually free, grasses are excellent fillers, plentiful enough to use generously and adventurously.

In early summer, grasses are soft green, and if picked then will retain green colour. Later in the season, they become various shades of beige or tan. Always pick grasses before the seed heads start to open; once they shatter, and the grain is shed from its cases, the heads become less attractive.

If you live or walk in the countryside, restrained gleaning of grains – barley, corn, millet, oats, rye and wheat – is useful. Barley is particularly delicate, with its long, graceful beard. Also, remember that grasses can be doubly useful in providing false stems. Always stick to the footpath or edge of the field; walking through the middle of a field of corn, though an attractively romantic idea, is very damaging to the crop.

Particularly lovely wild grasses are quaking grass (*Briza media*), so called because its pendulous, heart-shaped seed pods nod and tremble in the slightest breeze; and wild oat (*Avena fatua*), with its hair-like bristles.

In damp areas, look for sedges, rushes, and the huge sweet galingale (*Cyperus longus*), with stems 90cm (3ft) high. These grass-like members of the *Cyperaceae* family are relatives of the water-loving house plant, *Cyperus alternifolius*, and papyrus (*C. papyrus*), both of which can also be cut and air dried. Another inhabitant of wet lands is sweet grass, a 90cm-1.8m (3-6ft) high reed.

Bamboo is another unexpected member of the *Gramineae*. This garden escape can often be found in woods or by water. It is the bamboo foliage, which turns greeny pale beige, and twists as it dries, that is its main feature. Bamboo flowers are rarely produced and usually herald the demise of the plant.

Beachcombing

Shells, with their organic forms and muted colours, are naturally suitable containers or bases for dried flower displays. Because there is no need for water, even the flattest bivalve has potential. Use florist's foam impaled on prongs and a bit of mastic stuck underneath to stabilize the most contorted gastropod.

Shells with mother-of-pearl linings, such as ormers and abalones, are especially attractive, reflecting soft light onto the dried flowers. Tiny turk's-cap and button shells can be used in thick layers, like pebbles, to conceal florist's foam foundations. Like other aspects of summer holidays, however, the anticipation of collecting shells can be nicer than the reality. Many seaside resorts suffer from over-use, and the local fauna, like the local flora (see page 131) are in very low supply, if not extinct; some are protected by law.

Low tide reveals more treasures than high tide; local tackle shops should be able to provide you with tide time-tables, and perhaps guidance as to where the best beaches are. Early morning low tide, before the beaches become crowded, is ideal. Thoroughly scrub, then rinse the collected shells in several changes of water, to get rid of animal remains and sand deposits; you may have to boil the shells to eliminate any unpleasant smells.

Clams, mussels, winkles, ormers and cockles are temperate-climate possibilities. Tropical shells include huge fluted clams, splendid paper nautilus and conches. Coral is a traditional tropical ornament and depending on its shape, it can serve as the base for a display, or as the multi-stemmed 'trunk' of a dried-flower tree. Flat fan coral, used vertically, can make a miniature backdrop.

Coastal souvenir shops often have a selection of shells and coral for sale, many of which, ironically, are imported exotics. Seafood restaurants are as good a source as any for clam, cockle and mussel shells, for miniature containers; or scallop shells, for bases. (Teen-age children can find their parents taking 'doggy bags' home, whether of empty shells or leftover food, hideously embarrassing. If you intend to bring back booty, come equipped with a plastic bag.) Fishmongers are another good source, as are specialist craft shops and tropical fish shops, particularly those that supply tropical salt-water fish. Some natural history museums have shops which include shells and pieces of coral among their wares.

Pebbles These provide camouflage and stability for florist's foam foundations; larger stones can serve as bases themselves. Their weight is an advantage, in that they provide stability for lightweight displays, but a disadvantage if you have to carry what you collect over any distance, especially if you are travelling by plane. Nonetheless, a few special stones, like shells, can remind you of a pleasant foreign holiday or just an afternoon's walk along the coast.

Shingle beaches are a good source, as are the shallows and banks of swiftly flowing fresh water – mountain streams, for example. Water-washed stones tend to have a fluid smoothness, like tiny Henry Moore sculptures; some even have natural striations and holes.

Children and school holidays almost inevitably mean family trips to museums. Some geology museum shops sell a wide range of beautiful minerals, reasonably priced compared to similar ones sold in up-market department stores and gift shops. Geodes – hollow rocks, the inner cavity of which is lined with crystals, such as amethysts, or other matter – can make exquisite receptacles for dried flower displays. Thinly sliced sections of polished onyx, moss agate or rose quartz make bases, as do the naturally sculptured Mexican 'petal rose' and Sahara 'desert rose' rocks.

Geology museums and some craft shops also sell electric tumblers, which smooth and polish rough minerals, the final surface depending on

A single shell can bring to mind the pleasures of past summer vacations, and form the container of a tiny, dried-flower 'landscape'. Here, pink-dyed broom bloom and poppy seed heads, together with reindeer moss and bleached galax leaves, make a delicate display.

Sea holly, with its silvery, teasel-like heads and fiercely spiny, metallic bracts, air dries perfectly. Sea holly does grow wild, but in many places is becoming increasingly rare. There are, however, many Eryngium *species cultivated as ornamental herbaceous perennials and some are grown commercially for drying.*

the sharpness of the grit used. Although often used in the production of semi-precious jewellery, tumblers can produce polished pebbles for dried-flower displays. Polished semi-precious pebbles, and the more regular-shaped semi-precious 'eggs' are also available from some geology museum shops.

More mundanely, larger builder's merchants can supply granite chippings, washed gravel of various sizes and, sometimes, flints and marble chippings. Tropical aquarium suppliers have gravel of various types for fish tanks, and pet shops sell birdcage gravel. Dyed gravel, especially multi-colour gravel, is rarely sympathetic to the colours of natural dried material.

Driftwood This has a romantic ring to it, intimating distant origins and sea-swept voyages. In fact, finding natural driftwood on a crowded summer beach is almost as unlikely as finding a bottle with a message in it. (Searching a beach after a winter storm is more likely to be rewarding.) However, similarly twisted and naturally bleached wood occurs elsewhere, in windy, exposed sites; woodlands and orchards, for example. Water can cause wood to rot, but total submersion in water acts as a preservative. In marshes, rivers, lakes and bogs, the action of water and weather combine to give dead wood the characteristic patina of marine driftwood.

When water levels are low in summer, search the edges of woodland streams and lakes. Smooth branches or roots that have been submerged for most of the year become visible then. Bogwood – branches or roots preserved by organic acids in peat bogs – can be very attractive, and is found in the same environment as sphagnum moss (see page 102). Bogwood is also collected commercially, being much in demand as a decorative feature in tropical aquariums. Bogwood is usually sold by weight and a good tropical fish shop should have a wide range of shapes and sizes. Cork bark, used to line aquariums, makes an unusual base for a dried flower display.

In the southern states of America, cypress knees – the above-water portions of woody, buttress-like cypress roots – are collected then peeled and polished for sale.

Holiday Trophies

Summer holidays abroad are an avaricious time; duty-free goods, local crafts and, if you are a flower arranger, the temptation to bring back floral booty. Laws vary from country to country, but imported material is treated with much more circumspection than that taken from one part of the country to another, because authorities fear accidental importation of pests or diseases in the plant material. Material collected by the private individual is also more suspect than that imported commercially, as suppliers are aware of the complex regulations and problems, operate under licence and their premises are subject to inspection.

Most suspect of all are imported wild plants, which may contain virulent diseases and pests that attack related cultivated ones. Before bringing back any wild plants into England, you must obtain a licence, in advance, from the Ministry of Agriculture. Similar laws apply in many other countries. As well as the import laws of your own country, the export laws of the country in which the material is growing may prohibit export or even picking, especially if it is an endangered species.

Firstly, living plants, especially those with roots and soil attached, are more liable to be infected than the cut ones or those already dried. However, even dried material, such as the intricate protea flower head, can harbour tiny pests. Always declare what you have brought back, for your own peace of mind as much as anything else. Customs officials may want to know the method of drying; heat drying is more acceptable than air drying, for example.

Some plants, such as grape vines or any member of the potato (*Solanaceae*) family, are so risky in terms of potential diseases and pests, that they are totally prohibited in any form. Members of the daisy (*Compositae*), rose (*Rosaceae*), brassica (*Cruciferae*), grass (*Gramineae*), pea (*Leguminosae*) and carnation (*Caryophyllaceae*) families also cause particular concern, because so many related agricultural and ornamental crops are grown. Certain plants are allowable when imported from some countries, but not others; or at certain times of the year, but not others. There are leaflets available from government departments, setting out guidelines for importation.

Secondly, conservation, whether in your own or host country, is an equally important consideration, and also governed by law. State and national parks – often the venue for holidays – are under ever increasing human pressure, and although it is easy to justify taking the odd flower or two, on the grounds that it is only one or two, dozens of other flower arrangers may be harbouring similar dark thoughts.

Seaside holidays provide their own special temptation: sea holly, sea lavender, wild fennel, tansy, samphire and so on. Again, some are protected by law, but also looking in your heart of hearts, you probably have a good idea of how much or little harm you are doing, and whether the object of your desire is widespread, robust and capable of self perpetuation, or a dwindling species clinging on to life.

Thirdly, there are simple logistics to con-

sider. Fresh material is liable to wilt before it can be preserved, and there can be unexpected travel delays. Although dried material is relatively lightweight compared to its bulk, it can be very bulky and the number of pieces of baggage is usually limited when travelling by public transport. Flat material, such as palm leaves, is easier to pack between sheets of newspaper in the bottom of a suitcase than three-dimensional branches or flower heads. Carrying bunches of dried flowers or seed heads as hand baggage can be done, but terminals, airports and railway stations are very crowded places, and a certain amount of jostling is inevitable. If it is a long journey and the material is bulky, the limitations it places on such simple activities as reading or getting in and out of your seat can be annoying. There are very few restrictions on importing flower seeds from any country, and growing the desired plants from seed may be your only realistic alternative.

Fan coral from a tropical fish stockist forms the lacy backdrop for this 'maritime' display. Sea holly, sea lavender and silver- and pink-flowered xeranthemums continue the seaside theme, as does the flower-packed tropical conch shell.

Techniques – Using Desiccants

Of all the methods of preserving flowers, this one is most shrouded in mystery. Perhaps it is because the process takes place unseen – fresh flowers are literally buried from view – that an element of mystery is present. Desiccant-dried flowers are rarely available commercially, and then are quite expensive and already arranged – good reasons to dry your own. Flowers preserved in desiccant substantially retain their life-like form and colour, although some blue-based reds, such as red roses, do tend to darken, pinks tend to fade a little, and pure white flowers often take on creamy overtones, with age. Nonetheless, these variations are subtle ones, and desiccant-dried flowers can look amazingly life-like.

It is a very old method, practised by the ancient Egyptians, and one that has changed little since the following instructions were given in the eighteenth century book, *The Toilet of Flora*:

> *Take fine white sand, wash it repeatedly till it contains not the least earth or salt, then dry it for use. When thoroughly dry, fill a glass or stone jar half full of Sand in which stick the Flowers in their natural situation, and afterwards cover them gently with the same, about an eighth part of an inch above the Flower.*

Types of Desiccant
The most reliable, but most expensive, desiccant is silica gel. It is very quick acting, taking as little as a day with small flowers, such as violets, and usually no more than a week. Silica gel is available from chemists, as a sugar-like crystal, suitable for tougher flowers; or powder, suitable for delicate ones. You can pulverize the crystal form in a food processor or break it down with a rolling pin. There are also proprietary desiccants available, based on silica gel.

Household borax (less expensive and as effective as medical grade borax) and alum are also used. These are powdery and very light-weight, and take a week or more to dry material. Because they can be difficult to work into every crevice, and because they sometimes shrink and crack if in contact with a damp petal, they are often mixed, in equal proportions, with coarser-grained yellow cornmeal. If lumpy, sieve before use.

Sand and washing powder are other alternatives. The sand must be clean and fine grained. Some builder's merchants and garden centres sell packaged washed river sand. Otherwise, wash sand in a bucket or large sink bowl. Half-fill the container with sand, then run the water almost to the top, and remove any debris that floats to the surface. Wash again, with detergent, followed by several rinses in clear water. Dry in a low oven or outdoors in the sun, if weather permits. Sand is the heaviest of the desiccants, but also the easiest to work into every cavity in and around a flower. Sand tends to take longer than other desiccants to fully dry material, and can take a month or more.

Ideally, the more delicate the flower, the lighter the desiccant should be. You can, however, use any desiccant, provided you support the flower from underneath as you cover it, so the weight of the desiccant does not crush the flower.

Method
Flowers preserved in desiccant should be as fresh and dry as possible. Any trace of moisture on the petals causes discoloration and brown staining; moisture hidden in the centre of the flower leads to rot. Flowers picked slightly before fully open give better results than flowers at the peak of perfection, which often drop their petals or shatter once out of the desiccant.

Cut the stems to 2.5cm (1in) below the head, so the flower can fit into the lidded box. You can later insert the remaining stems, with a drop of glue, into hollow false stems, once the flowers are dried. Alternatively, immediately wire the cut-off stems with short stub wires, which can be attached to longer wires at a later date. Either insert the wire into the stumpy stem, which shrinks around the wire as it dries, or stick a wire through the calyx, then bend it upright.

Larger stems of flowers, such as delphiniums, can be preserved on their sides, but need a long box. It helps to use several upright, notched pieces of cardboard to rest the stems on as you work the desiccant round the flower, otherwise the flowers on the underside tend to get crushed.

The desiccant has to be totally dry before use; silica gel is sold with moisture-sensitive paper which turns blue when the desiccant is totally dry, or the crystals themselves change from blue to pink if damp. If they are damp, dry them in a shallow roasting tin or other container in a low oven before use.

Cover the bottom of the container, such as a shoe box, biscuit tin or plastic freezer carton, with a 1-2.5cm (½-1in) layer of desiccant. Coffee tins are ideal for individual flowers, such as large roses, and yoghurt cartons or paper cups are fine for smaller individual flowers. If possible, do one type of flower per container, as drying times for flowers vary. Flat-faced flowers, such as pansies, single clematis and cosmos can be dried face down.

More 'three-dimensional' flowers, such as roses and dahlias, should be dried face up, so that gravity helps fill all the crevices with desiccant. You can do several flowers in a layer, but make sure they do not touch each other. Make sure, too, that the petals are in their natural position, as they cannot be adjusted afterwards. Use a pointed stick, paintbrush handle or toothpick to adjust the petals, if necessary.

Every bit of flower surface must be in contact with the desiccant. Try to evenly build up the levels of desiccant around and inside the flower, to prevent crushing the flower outwards with the weight of the desiccant. This is more important with heavy desiccants, such as sand and silica gel crystals, than with lightweight desiccants, such as soap powder.

Begin covering the flower in desiccant, either spooning it around and into the flower, or sifting it over the flower, letting the desiccant

Preserving roses in a desiccant

Cut the stems, leaving 2.5 cm (1 in) attached to the flower. If wished, insert a short stub wire into the cut-off stem. Otherwise, the flower head can be wired once dried.

Cover the bottom of the container with a 1-2.5 cm (½-1 in) layer of desiccant. Place the flowers in the container, making sure they are not touching one another. Begin spooning over the desiccant, building it up evenly as you proceed.

Make sure that every bit of the flower is covered with desiccant, and that there are no air pockets. Use a fine brush or tooth pick to work the desiccant into every crevice.

133

The lenten rose, Helleborus orientalis, *can be successfully preserved in a desiccant.*

run between your fingers. Cover the flower thoroughly, working the desiccant into every crevice, especially where the petals join the base of the stem. Light-weight desiccants are sometimes hard to move into position, and a fine camel-hair brush helps. (You can use the brush afterwards, to dust off any grains of desiccant clinging to the flowers).

Continue filling the container, tapping it from time to time to help settle the desiccant. Several layers of flowers can be treated in a single container, depending on its depth and the size of the flowers. Cover the top (or only) layer of flowers with at least 2.5cm (1in) of desiccant, then tightly cover with the container lid to keep out atmospheric moisture.

Gentle heat speeds up the action of borax and sand; you can place the filled container in a very low oven, 110°F/gas¼/40°C – in which case leave the lid off, to allow the moisture to escape – for an hour or so. The desiccant can also be warmed immediately before use. Placing the filled container over a radiator or in an airing cupboard is another way of speeding up the process.

Timing

The time taken varies, according to the desiccant and size, water content and thickness of the material. Double flowers and those with intricate petals take longer to dry than single ones. When roughly the right amount of time

has elapsed, remove the cover, tilt the box and begin pouring out the desiccant into another box. As the first flower appears, catch it in your hand, check for 'done-ness'. It should feel dry and papery. If it does not, return it and the desiccant to the box, and put it away for a few more days. If it does, carefully pour out the remainder of the desiccant, retrieving the flowers as they appear. You can bury a 'test' flower just below the surface for easy retrieval without having to disturb the others. Mark its position with an upright toothpick.

Storage

Theoretically, you can leave flowers in corn-meal, borax, sand or washing powder, until needed for use, although those left too long in silica gel become unnaturally dark and brittle. In practice, removing the flowers as soon as fully dried allows you to put a fresh lot of flowers in for treatment. Desiccants can be re-used indefinitely, provided they are sieved to remove any plant particles and lumps, then dried thoroughly in shallow roasting tins in a low oven, 250°F/gas½/120°C, for about thirty minutes.

Flowers preserved in desiccant, particularly in silica gel, are even sensitive to the atmospheric moisture, and sometimes go limp and collapse in humid environments. Such flowers are often displayed in airtight glass cases for this reason.

Flowers Suitable for Drying in Desiccants

Anemone	Hellebore	Polyanthus
Broom	Hemerocallis	Pot marigold
Camellia	Hollyhock	Rose
Canterbury bell	Hyacinth	Rudbeckia
Carnation	Larkspur	Snowball bush
Clematis	Lilac	Sweet pea
Columbine	Lily of the valley	Sweet William
Cosmos	Marigold	Violet
Dahlia	Narcissus	Wallflower
Delphinium	Paeony	Water lily
Forsythia	Pansy	Zinnia
Gentian	Philadelphus	

Preserving with Glycerine

Glycerine mixed with water is used primarily for the preservation of foliage, both evergreen and deciduous, but some berries and a few flowers can also be preserved with glycerine. The process is a simple one, worth doing because the material retains much of its natural shape and three-dimensional quality, and commercially glycerined foliage is very rare. As foliage often makes or breaks an arrangement, having a good supply of your own glycerined material is doubly important, and it can add personality to a display otherwise dependent on conventional, unmemorable, store-bought dried flowers. With glycerined material, the water in the plant cells is gradually replaced by the glycerine, which acts as a preservative.

Glycerine is expensive – though cheaper if bought in bulk – but a little goes a long way, and glycerined material lasts for years. Antifreeze, which is less expensive, can sometimes be used instead, particularly with laurel, box, elaeagnus, privet, mahonia and ivy. With other material, it is largely a case of trial and error. Antifreeze is dyed in one of several bright colours, according to brand, none of which affects the finished colour of the foliage.

Whole stems, such as those of beech and eucalyptus, can be treated, or individual large leaves, such as Fatsia japonica or Aspidistra elatior. Some plants are capable of taking up glycerine over larger lengths than others. Branches of Cotoneaster horizontalis, escallonia and beech can be preserved up to 90cm (3ft) long. Ivy, Griselinia littoralis and Choisya ternata can only be preserved in short lengths. Again, it is largely a matter of experimenting. In the case of foliage 'on the stem', you can display the material as it is being preserved, and enjoy watching the process take place. The leaf veins tend to turn a deeper colour, as the glycerine is taken up, then the colouring spreads through the leaf tissue. Once stems of foliage are fully preserved, they can be used in displays of fresh flowers as well as dried, as the stems take up no further water. It is also possible to preserve single leaves or short stems, such as those of camellia or evergreen magnolia, then use them to reconstruct large branches.

Unlike dried or desiccated material, glycerined material tends to change colour, usually to shades ranging from silvery grey to almost black. You can partially control the colour change by the amount of light in which the material is glycerined; the darker the conditions, the darker the material tends to be. How long you leave the material in glycerine can also affect the colour. Partially preserved eucalyptus, for example, has veining of rich purple against basically blue-grey leaves. Fully preserved eucalyptus has even tones of bronze or purple. Partially preserved escallonia is particularly attractive, being a mixture of deep green and bronze, but partially preserved material does not last indefinitely. Sometimes there is a variation in colour depending on the preservative used: Fatsia japonica and Helleborus corsicus turn mid-brown when preserved with glycerine, but a darker, richer brown when preserved in antifreeze.

The texture of fully glycerined foliage is supple and leathery, often with a shiny, polished surface. It is tough and less liable to damage than brittle dried material, can be dusted or wiped without damage, and re-used again and again.

Methods Collecting the material at its optimum stage of growth is very important. The leaves must be fully mature and capable of taking up sap, not young and soft. On the other hand, left too late in the season, leaves start to dry out and no amount of glycerine can preserve them. Midsummer to early autumn is generally the best time to harvest material for glycerining. Even evergreen foliage, which is commonly thought of as being much the same all year round, is best collected in summer. In the winter months, the sap barely rises, so the glycerine would be equally slow; and in spring, unsuitable soft growth is produced. Deciduous foliage which has begun to change colour in autumn is beautiful but equally unsuitable, as the corky abscision layer has already formed between the leaf stalk and twig, blocking the intake of sap and, therefore, any preserving fluid.

The time it takes for material to be fully preserved varies, from a week or less in the

135

Preserving foliage in glycerine

Prepare the woody stems, so they can fully absorb the glycerine and water mixture. Remove the bottom 2.5-5 cm (1-2 in.) of bark, and hammer or split the wood. If some time has elapsed between initial cutting and preparation, re-cut the stem.

Thoroughly mix hot water with one third to one half its own volume of glycerine. Place the selected material in a heavy, narrow-diameter container, and pour in the glycerine mixture to a depth of 5 cm (2 in).

For thick, leathery leaves, such as ivy, Fatsia japonica, *and bergenia, place the leaves in a shallow, flat container, such as a roasting pan. Fill with the glycerine mixture and make sure the leaves are fully covered with the liquid, pushing them down from time to time as necessary.*

case of *Cotoneaster horizontalis* and escallonia, to six weeks, in the case of *Fatsia japonica* and *Prunus laurocerasus.* Generally, the larger and thicker the leaf, the longer the preserving process takes.

There are two basic methods: submerging the cut end of a stem in a mixture of glycerine (or antifreeze) and water, and allowing the stem to absorb the liquid; or submerging large, single leaves completely in a mixture of glycerine (or antifreeze) and water, which is absorbed through the pores. Heating the water to boiling point helps the solution to more quickly penetrate thick, woody stems; do not heat the glycerine, as it is combustible, and use antifreeze cold. Soft-stemmed material should be put in a lukewarm or cold solution. Some people use equal parts glycerine or antifreeze and water, while other people use one part glycerine or antifreeze to two parts water. The latter is more economical, though the former is marginally quicker acting.

There is no point in preserving diseased or insect-damaged leaves or branches of overcrowded leaves. Carefully go over the material beforehand, thinning leaves as necessary, and pruning the branch to give a pleasing over-all form. Speed is of the essence, and once foliage has wilted, it is unlikely to be able to take up the glycerine (or antifreeze) mixture. You can sometimes revive wilted foliage by re-cutting the stem and giving it a long drink of water before placing in preservative. It often helps to re-cut the stem in any case, even if only a few minutes elapse between the initial cut and placing in preservative. Prepare woody stems as you would do for fresh arrangements, stripping the bark for 2.5-5cm (1-2in) and hammering or slitting them, so they can more easily absorb the mixture.

Mix the thick glycerine and water thoroughly, so the glycerine does not settle on the bottom; you can either stir it or put into a container with a tight-fitting lid and shake vigorously. To maximize the use of a limited amount of glycerine, select a heavy, narrow container — narrow because less solution is then needed, and heavy so that it does not tip over from the weight of large branches. You can place the smaller container inside a bucket or other larger container, and balance or rest the branches against the rim. Keep the material somewhere warm and dry, and where air circulates freely. Pour the solution to a depth of 5cm (2in). Check the level of the solution from time to time, topping up with more hot liquid as necessary and making sure that it does not run out before the material is fully preserved.

The process is complete when the foliage has changed colour evenly throughout, and is smooth and flexible to the touch. If the upper leaves, particularly of large branches, become dry and brittle part way through, the solution is not being absorbed quickly enough. Apply the solution externally to these leaves, on their upper and under surfaces, using a cloth, cotton wool or kitchen paper. Apply again, from time to time, as necessary. If beads of solution form on the leaves, especially the tips, the foliage has been in the liquid too long. Remove and gently wipe away the beads, using a damp cloth, allow to dry fully, then store or use the foliage. Unabsorbed glycerine can be re-used, even if discoloured. Strain and boil it, then store in a covered jar or re-use immediately.

Thick leaves, such as those of ivy, bergenia and Fatsia japonica often respond better to being submerged in a half water, half glycerine or antifreeze solution. Other suitable candidates for submersion are aspidistra, mahonia, hosta and whitebeam. Push them down from time to time, to make sure they are fully submerged. Use a shallow, flat container, such as a roasting tray or soup bowl. When the leaf colour and texture is right, drain on newspaper for a couple of days, wash with mild soap and water, then rinse and dry thoroughly.

Plant Material for Glycerining

PLANTS	PRESERVED COLOUR	PLANTS	PRESERVED COLOUR	PLANTS	PRESERVED COLOUR
Suitable Foliage		Fatsia japonica	brown shades	**Suitable Berries**	
		Garrya elliptica	dark brown		
Acer spp	gold/brown	Griselinia littoralis	deep brown	Hedera helix	green/black
Alchemilla mollis	pale brown	Hedera helix	mid-brown	Rosa spp	deep orange
Aspidistra elatior	straw	Helleborus corsicus	pale brown	Rubus (blackberry)	purple black
Aucuba japonica	brown/black	Hosta ssp	beige	Sorbus aucuparia	deep orange
Berberis (evergreen) spp	deep brown	Laurus nobilis	grey green		
Bergenia cordifolia	deep brown	Ligustrum ssp	mid-brown	*Treat foliage and berries together, if wished	
Betula spp	yellow/brown	Lonicera pileata	mid-brown		
Buxus sempervirens	pale beige	Magnolia grandiflora	deep brown		
Camellia japonica	deep brown	Mahonia spp	brown shades		
Castanea sativa	pale brown	Paeonia spp	grey green		
Chamaecyparis	red-brown	Phormium tenax	beige		
Choisya ternata	beige	Pittosporum spp	rich brown		
Cotoneaster horizontalis	deep brown	Polygonatum multiflorum	creamy beige		
Cupressus spp	mid-brown	Prunus laurocerasus	brown/black		
Elaeagnus macrophylla	pale beige	Quercus spp	red/brown	**Suitable Flowers**	
Elaeagnus pungens		Rhododendron spp	deep brown		
'Maculata'	yellow/brown	Rosmarinus officinalis	silver grey	Astrantia major	beige
Erica spp	red-brown	Ruscus aculeatus	pale beige	Clematis vitalba	pinky silver
Escallonia spp	bronze	Sorbus aria	mid-brown	Moluccella laevis	pale beige
Eucalyptus spp	grey/purple	Viburnum rhytidophyllum	brown shades	Polygonum spp	dark red
Fagus sylvatica	rich brown	Viburnum tinus	rich brown	Tilia spp	green/beige

Making Potpourris

Potpourris – fragrant mixtures of dried flowers, foliage, fixatives and spices – are commercially available, but making your own is easy and enjoyable. If you have a flower garden, home-made potpourri preserves the memory of its summer glory through the winter months indoors. Potpourris also make splendid gifts, whether presented in a sachet, home-made potpourri pillow, in a pretty glass brandy snifter or bowl covered with gauze or even cling film.

There are two types of potpourri: wet or moist, and dry. The former, based on layering the partially dried material in salt, then adding spices and fixatives, is the more 'authentic', as the literal translation for the word potpourri is 'rotted pot'. The following is a typical Victorian recipe for moist potpourri:

'The roses used should be just blown, of the sweetest smelling kinds, gathered in as dry a state as possible. After each gathering, spread out the petals on a sheet of paper and leave until free from all moisture; then place a layer of petals in the jar, sprinkling with coarse salt; then another layer and salt, alternating until the jar is full. Leave for a few days, or until a broth is formed; then incorporate thoroughly, and add more petals and salt, mixing daily for a week , when fragrant gums and spices should be added, such as benzoin, storax, cassia buds, cinnamon, clove, cardamom and vanilla bean.
Mix again and leave for a few days, when add essential oil of jasmine, violet, tuberose and attar of roses, together with a hint of ambergris or musk, in mixture with the flower attars to fix the odour. Spices, such as cloves, should be sparingly used. A rose potpourri thus combined, without parsimony in supplying the flower attars, will be found in the fullest sense a joy forever.'

(The Gardener's Story, or Pleasures and Trials of an Amateur Gardener, by George H. Ellwanger.

Dry Potpourri This is easier to make and much more attractive to look at. Rose petals usually form the basis, as they are colourful and tend to retain their original fragrance. Among the most heavily fragrant are the cabbage or Provence rose, Rosa centifolia; and the damask rose, R. damascena. Roses with little or no original fragrance obviously remain that way. Some lavender, too, is more fragrant than others; French lavender, Lavandula stoechas, is intensely fragrant, but less hardy than others, as is woolly lavender, L. lanata, from Spain. Unfortunately, many richly coloured varieties tend to be less rich in fragrance.

Any colourful flowers are suitable, however, and if they lack scent, fragrance can be added in the form of essential oils and spices. Although summer flowers traditionally form the bulk of potpourris, spring flowers such as wallflowers, narcissus and hyacinths can also be used. Dry them when they flower, and store for use later in the season.

Ambergris, civet and musk are the traditional natural fixatives, which absorb and retain the volatile fragrances of the flowers and essential oils, but today powdered dried orris root or gum benzoin, in resin form, is more commonly used. Spices vary according to 'taste', but include allspice, cinnamon, nutmeg, mace and cloves. Oriental mixtures sometimes include cardamom, coriander and anise. As with cooking, freshly ground spices have a clearer and more intense aroma than those bought in powdered form.

Strips of dried orange or lemon peel can also be added. Peel the fresh fruit leaving as little pith attached as possible, then place them in a dry, warm, well-ventilated spot, or put them in a very low oven to dry out. You might want to try strips of lime or grapefruit peel as an unusual alternative.

Essential oils include rose oil, citronella, rose geranium oil, bergamot oil, lavender oil, eucalyptus oil, almond oil, patchouli, lemon verbena oil, gardenia oil and cedarwood oil. Always add oil with caution; you can add another drop if necessary, but you cannot remove excess, and too much essential oil may transform a subtle, natural fragrance into a coarse one. The strength and quality of essential oils can vary from one source to another, so again, err on the side of caution. As a general rule, start with one drop of essential oil per two cups of dried flowers, and add more as necessary. There is also a ready-mixed essence of potpourri available from some stockists.

Method Pick the petals and any aromatic leaves on a dry day, but before the heat of the sun causes the essential oils to volatize and evaporate; the more you can smell the flowers, the less fragrance remains for your potpourri! Small flowers can be left whole; strip the petals from larger flowers, and the leaves from the stems. Leave a few tiny rose buds whole, however, more for appearance than for scent. Either hang them upside down to dry, or dry in a desiccant, such as sand, silica gel or borax. Tear larger leaves, such as those of bergamot, into small strips.

Lay the petals, leaves or flowers in a single layer on absorbent kitchen paper on a tray, shallow rimmed dish or even shoe box lid. Alternatively, use small mesh wire screens, or cheesecloth tightly stretched across a wooden frame. Dry the flowers and foliage separately, according to species, as the time taken for drying varies, according to the thickness and size of the material, and its natural moisture content. Place them somewhere well ventilated, warm and dry, but out of direct sunlight. If you are drying them outdoors, and nights tend to be cool and damp, bring them in each evening, and return them the following day, weather permitting. (Beware of windy or changeable weather, though!) Other good places include an airing cupboard, attic, or over a night store heater or radiator. Do not dry them in an oven, or in front of an electric room heater, as they are liable to cook rather than dry, and the volatile oils will be destroyed.

Turn the flowers or petals over from time to time, and leave until they turn leathery, then are literally crispy, and reduced by over half in bulk. Ten days to two weeks is usually necessary, depending on the weather and material. Dry aromatic leaves in the same way, but if you are in a hurry, hang bunches of stems upside-down to dry, then strip the leaves.

Making potpourri

Spread petals from the chosen flowers in a single layer to dry on absorbent paper on a tray or rack. Place somewhere airy, warm and dry, but out of direct sunlight. Treat aromatic leaves in the same way, although small bunches can be hung upside-down to dry, then the leaves stripped when fully dried.

When the petals from the various flowers are dry and papery to the touch, combine them in a bowl, together with strips of dried orange peel, if wished. Small dried flower heads, such as rose buds, are an optional but particularly attractive extra.

Add essential oils sparingly, drop by drop, together with freshly ground spices, such as allspice and cinnamon. A small amount of gum benzoin acts as a fixative, retaining the volatile fragrances of the other ingredients.

139

To add a bit of visual interest to potpourri, attach a cluster of dried flowers or even dried grasses to the container. Fine ribbon and potpourri make another inherently attractive combination; with woven containers, such as the Victorian Leedsware shown, you can weave ribbon through the lattice-work.

Recipes

There are many recipes for dry potpourris, and an almost infinite number of variations, rather like cookery recipes for popular dishes. The following are just basic guides, springboards for experimentation. Combine all the ingredients, adding the oil last, then mix thoroughly and put in a sealed container. Leave for three to six weeks in a dry, warm, dark place, shaking and stirring the mixture from time to time.

Basic Mixed Flower Potpourri

1½ cups dried rose petals
1 cup dried lavender flowers
1 cup dried lemon verbena leaves
1½ tsp cinnamon
1½ tsp allspice
1½ tsp ground cloves
¼ oz gum benzoin
1 drop rose oil

Basic Rose Potpourri

1½ cups dried rose petals
¼ tsp cinnamon
¼ tsp ground cloves
¼ tsp dried peppermint leaves
¼ tsp allspice
1 tsp dried orris root
2 drops rose oil

Basic Lemon Potpourri

1½ cups dried lemon balm leaves
1½ cups dried lemon verbena leaves
1 large strip dried lemon peel
1½ cups dried chamomile flowers
1½ cups dried pot marigold flowers
1½ cups dried African marigold flowers
½ cup orris root powder
4 drops lemon oil, lime oil or lemon verbena oil

Basic Lavender Potpourri

1 cup dried lavender flowers
2 tbls powdered orris root
1 small strip dried lemon peel
2 tbls dried mint leaves
1 tbls dried rosemary leaves
1 tbls dried lemon balm leaves
½ tsp gum benzoin
1 drop oil of lavender

Treat potpourris like perfume, exposing them to the air from time to time for intense bursts of fragrance. There are special china or brass potpourri jars available, with wide necks and perforated lids, but any lidded jar will suffice. Potpourris which have lost their fragrance can be revived with a few drops of essential oil, or a mixture as close as possible to the original one. Some specialists sell potpourri reviver essence.

Lavender, though intensely fragrant, can look dusty on its own. Here, dried, deep-red rosebuds and rich purple mallow add contrasting colour and scale.

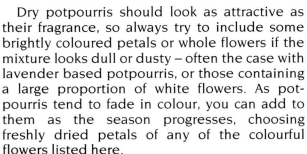

Dry potpourris should look as attractive as their fragrance, so always try to include some brightly coloured petals or whole flowers if the mixture looks dull or dusty – often the case with lavender based potpourris, or those containing a large proportion of white flowers. As potpourri tend to fade in colour, you can add to them as the season progresses, choosing freshly dried petals of any of the colourful flowers listed here.

Flowers Suitable for Potpourris

Fragrant flowers
Buddleia
Chamomile
Clove pinks (Dianthus caryophyllus)
Cotton lavender
Heliotrope
Honeysuckle
Jasmine
Lavender
Lily
Lily of the valley
Lime
Mignonette
Mimosa
Philadelphus
Rose
Sweet pea
Sweet woodruff
Sweet violet (Viola odorata)
Tansy
Tobacco plant
Verbena
Wallflower

Flowers for additional colour
Celosia
Clematis
Cornflower
Delphinium

Goldenrod
Helichrysum
Hydrangea
Larkspur
Marigold
Paeony
Pansy
Pot marigold
Salvia
Statice
Yarrow
Zinnia

Herbs
Artemisia
Bay
Bergamot
Costmary
Scented-leaved geraniums
Lemon balm
Lemon thyme
Lemon verbena
Mint
Myrtle
Rosemary
Sage
Sweet basil
Sweet marjoram
Tarragon

Styles of Arrangement

Large-scale displays can be splendid but present two metaphorical hurdles: cost and structural stability. Dried flowers do cost more than fresh ones, because more time and effort is involved in their preservation. Flowers often shrink during the preserving process, so more material is needed to give the same bulk as the equivalent amount of fresh flowers.

One solution is to use as much wild or garden material as possible. The branches of almost any woody shrubs or trees can be called into use (see pages 65-67 for ideas.) For example, sink several leafless, angular branches of robinia in a terra cotta pot half-filled with quick-setting plaster. Spray the branches white, if wished, and when the plaster dries, cover it with florist's foam impaled on florist's frogs. Build up a dense cluster of dried flowers at the base, to conceal the plaster and create 'ground cover' under the tree. The finished effect is one of largesse, although only a modest amount of dried material is needed. You can also stud the branches with single or small clusters of dried flowers, held on with a dab of quick-drying glue. Dried, full-length stems of bamboo are another brilliant stand-by for large-scale displays. They are subtly beautiful on their own, or clusters of dried flowers could be added to the bamboo for flashes of colour.

Pedestals are an old-fashioned way of adding height and scale; modern equivalents include chimney pots, old wooden high chairs and natural or brightly painted wooden 'bar' stools. The traditional lollipop tree, shown on page 81, operates on the principle of elevating flowers; you could make the main stem head height, and increase its diameter and that of the globe accordingly.

Consider using a moss pole, or a group or row of moss poles, to support a generous display of dried flowers. A tripod of bamboo poles can support a flower-covered florist's foam globe resting in its crook. Or use flexible plastic

An old-fashioned woven laundry basket filled to the brim with dried flowers, and embellished with a dried flower swag, makes a glorious large-scale display. An unseen wire-mesh netting support fills most of the space in the basket, so that even quite short-stemmed subjects can be used. With large-scale displays, plenty of space is needed, so the display can be seen to best advantage, and the risk of accidental damage is minimal.

142

trellis, such as that used for supporting clematis, to form a cylindrical support. The dried material can be worked through the trellis as well as onto a florist's foam globe or cone impaled on the top. Classical, free-standing, wooden trellis frameworks in pyramidal design are available. These are used mainly for training ivies in formal gardens, but could form a framework for a magnificent large-scale dried flower display. On a more modest budget, some oriental stores sell simple bamboo 'trees', with main trunks and side 'branches' of bamboo. Wire chunks of florist's foam onto the tree framework, and decorate with dried flowers, grasses or seed pods.

An empty woven laundry basket or terra cotta 'Ali Baba' pot can be filled with crumpled newspaper, then covered with wire mesh netting and topped with a generous layer of dried flowers. An old wooden wheelbarrow or antique doll's pram can be treated in the same way, with a foundation of crumpled wire netting over newspaper. When, as in these cases, the flowers are only skin deep but meant to give the impression of great depth, there must be no break in the 'skin', or the game is given away. Make sure that the flowers wrap round into every corner.

Lavishly decorating a life-size statue is an opportunity denied to most of us, but an old-fashioned dressmaker's dummy could be given a lush garland of dried flowers, or a flower-covered globe instead of a head. A modern, mesh dressmaker's dummy could sprout a dense outer covering of dried flowers, a floral garment in the truest sense of the word. If space allowed, a garden arch or trellis – in a sun room or conservatory, perhaps, or an arch dividing living and dining areas – could be festooned with dried flowers. 'Borrowing' the stability of another structure, such as a dressmaker's dummy or garden arch, is always a safe approach, as dried flowers are too light to destabilize a basically steady support. Do not be afraid to 'borrow' the beauty of a large-scale support at the same time: a huge weeping fig could carry clusters of dried flowers, wired to the branches, for a special dinner party or social event.

Country Casual

Displays of dried flowers that appear casual can take hours of careful work to contrive, rather like the casual appearance of a top fashion model's hair style, for example, or the casual folds in a couturier dress. With dried flowers, a successful country casual effect is usually the result of a thoughtful selection of material, container and setting.

Material The type of material should ideally be local, whether wild or cultivated in one's own garden, and serve as reference to the immediate environment. By the sea, this could be wild fennel, sea holly, sea lavender and seakale seed pods, displayed simply in a salt-glaze jar. (Ironically, you may have to buy commercially grown material, but the finished effect will be the same!) Obviously, those who live in the country or suburbs have a wider choice than urbanites, but even in cities the dark-brown seed heads from buddleias, which grow in the most unexpected urban spots, and the docks and thistles from vacant plots and building sites, can serve as a starting point.

Supplementary, bought-in flowers should be believable as gleanings from a day's outing in the countryside. Material that instantly declares itself as exotic – for example, banksias or proteas in a northern temperate climate – may strike a false note. So would dried, long-stemmed roses – so obviously the products of commercial greenhouses – and sports, such as contorted willow and contorted hazel, sophisticated, but inherently unnatural. Using dyed material in a country casual display might be philosophically wrong, but it can be successful if the colours are natural looking. Blatantly dyed material – for example, glixia with bright blue or fuchsia-coloured stems – are not suitable.

Arrangements Informality and fussiness are mutually exclusive, and restricting the number of different types of dried flowers is usually more successful than following the 'one of each' approach. There are exceptions: dozens of different species of wild grasses, in shades of beige and tan, for example, 'read' as a single texture. Material collected from a single stretch of hedgerow or a single woodland clearing

'Country casual' has become the banner under which such widely disparate items as tweed skirts, bedroom suites and china sets are sold. With dried flowers or, indeed, any flower arrangement, the idea is that the display does not look arranged, but rather, about to be arranged. Humble containers, such as stoneware kitchen storage jars or the wooden trug shown, help emphasize the feeling of informality.

A pretty trio of old-fashioned posies, ranging in size from miniature to quite substantial. It can take only a few minutes and ribbon to transform a store-bought mixed bunch into a 'personalized' posy, and even the addition of half a dozen wild grasses or dried garden flowers can make a world of difference.

tends to combine together quite naturally.

If you can combine material in various stages of maturity – cornflower buds and flowers, for example, or green and tan teasels – nature is more closely approximated than if every flower or pod is identical. Nature and art part company, however, where damaged or broken material is concerned, and there is no room in a country casual display for anything obviously defective.

Abundance is another requisite to a successful country casual display, and one which looks as if each flower has been signed for in triplicate is unlikely to convey a casual feeling. This does not mean that displays have to be big, merely that they have to appear generous.

Dried flowers, seed pods and foliage resting in a woven wicker or wooden garden basket, as if newly collected and about to be arranged, is a traditional country casual approach. The sideboard in a dining-room or the counter of a country-style kitchen would be suitable settings. In a generously proportioned entrance hall, the trug or basket could rest on the floor, as if put there momentarily. (The presence of dogs or boisterous children make floor-level displays risky, and resting the trug on an old-fashioned wooden high chair or shelf might be better.)

Hanging dried flowers up as if in the process of being dried, is another country casual approach, particularly useful if space at ground or table level is limited or vulnerable. A coat hook, cup hook or picture hook can provide support for a single bunch. For a multiple display, specialist kitchen shops offer a range of pot rails, usually of steel. Straight bars and semi-circular rails can be fixed to a wall, and bunches hung from them. If room allows, a large, circular pot rail on chains could be hung from the ceiling, then hung with several bunches of dried flowers, rather like a floral equivalent of a chandelier.

A floppy, woven straw shopping basket could be filled with dried flowers, then hung on a wall or old-fashioned, bentwood coat stand – again, the sense of the flowers being in transit adds to the informality. African woven rope satchels are available in an amazing range of colours and subtly striped colour combinations. The satchels are handcrafted but not overbearingly ethnic, and would be ideal for such a display.

Country casual floral displays tend to be reinforced by a setting which invokes country life – scrubbed pine, tiny floral printed wallpapers and fabrics, hand-made pottery – but the country casual approach can also be refreshingly effective in a modern interior. A log basket brimming with dried flowers and grasses can be a most dramatic focal point in a stark, white room.

Making Posies

'To get half a dozen of mixed flowers, bundled together anyhow, and to go into good company with such a nosegay in these days, is looked upon as certainly not a mark of high breeding.'

So warned Godey's *Lady's Book* in 1855. Although nosegays, or posies, are no longer automatically carried to social events, a posy should be a considered arrangement, especially if it is a gift. It makes a pleasant change from the usual elongated, flat-backed bouquet. A posy can be immediately placed in a tall container, such as a bud vase, for an instant display, without any need for further arrangement. (For collectors, there are elaborate Victorian posy holders, of china, amber, cut steel, mother of pearl or precious metal. Some have collapsible legs which form a supporting tripod for when the owner's hands are occupied.)

Posies can be wired or unwired, and take minutes or hours to construct. For a formal Victorian posy, built up as a tight dome of concentric floral circles around a central rose bud or tight cluster of buds, wiring gives a more controlled result, though it is time consuming. With silver reel wire, wire sufficient small bunches of flowers or florets to construct the posy, keeping the colours in separate piles. (Every ring can be a different colour, or colours can be repeated; outer rings obviously require more material than inner ones.) Tape each bunch to a stub wire, which will form a composite handle, but do not tape the entire length of the stub wire, or the handle will be thick and ungainly.

Assembly Make up the first small dense circle of contrasting flowers around and slightly lower than the central focal point. Continue making larger, lower circles, holding the developing posy in one hand. Each successive circle will require a longer length of stub wire and meet the central handle at a sharper angle. As you proceed, secure the stub wires with reel wire, to form a handle. When the desired diameter is reached – 15-20 cm (6-8in) – trim the stub wires to 10-15cm (4-6in) long. Tape the handle, then slip a starched lace or *broderie anglaise* frill round the rim and fix with silver reel wire. Finish the

Making formal posies

Begin by wiring small, tight bunches of flowers, using silver reel wire. Keep in mind that outer rings require more material than inner ones. Make up the first small, dense circle around and slightly lower than the central cluster or bud.

Make larger, lower circles until the desired diameter is reached. Each successive circle will need longer stub wires. As you proceed, wire the individual stub wires together, to form a central handle.

Tape the handle with florist's tape, then slip on a broderie anglaise *or lace frill, with a paper backing, if necessary. Conceal the florist's tape with a ribbon, wrapped diagonally round the handle. Add a bow and trailing streamers, if wished. The finished posy is shown on page 149.*

handle with diagonally wrapped ribbon, adding a bow with trailers, if wished.

There are easier methods. One is to use a florist's bridey: a plastic handle fitted with a cage-like structure at the top, into which florist's foam fits. For a Victorian posy, place the handle in a heavy bottle or jar and work from the central bud outwards, as above. Strong-stemmed material can be inserted directly into the florist's foam, although the end result will be looser and less dense than a wired posy, and covering the florist's foam with a thin layer of sphagnum moss first is a good idea. As well as a design based on concentric rings, a formal posy could be built up of evenly distributed poppy heads, dyer's greenwood or rose buds, against a low-key background, such as tightly-packed creamy white statice.

Informal posies have a different charm, and can consist of a single species, perhaps with a contrasting frill of ferns or glycerined cypress or beech leaves; or several types of flowers. If using a bridey, establish the general roundness and density with a filler, such as lady's mantle or cow parsley, then add more well defined material, perhaps larger flowers, towards the centre. Informal posies should be slightly irregular and lacy round the edges, though informality is no excuse for lopsidedness.

Closest to the romantic conception of a posy gathered fresh from the garden is an informal bouquet, built up in one hand. Start with the longest flowers in the centre and gradually add more flowers evenly round it, with the flower heads turning out from the centre. Bind each stem in with silver reel wire as you increase the girth of the posy. Once the desired diameter is reached, gradually decrease the girth of the lower flowers, for a rounded effect. Secure the wire, then cut the stems, and conceal the wire with a bow or raffia.

Small posies, or tussy mussies, were originally carried to ward off disease and disguise unpleasant smells. Continue the tradition with tiny sprigs of dried herbs, such as lavender, rosemary or sage, wrapped with wire and worn as an unusual, aromatic corsage on a lapel in the place of jewellery. Alternatively, display in a wine glass or egg cup.

A Victorian posy composed of concentric circles of bleached hair grass, red-dyed broom bloom and oat grass. Rose buds form the central focal point and additional buds add colour in the outer ring. Tiny amounts of gypsophila, quaking grass and bleached canary grass are worked in at regular intervals, to contribute to the richly detailed finished effect.

GLOSSARY

Tools and Materials

Exquisite displays of dried flowers can be produced, using just a pair of kitchen scissors. Having more suitable tools, though, saves time and helps prevent frustration and broken or otherwise damaged material. (Using the right tools also means that you do not ruin unsuitable tools through misuse.) Hardware stores, garden and DIY centres, and florists are the major sources of supplies, but if you are very keen, it is worth approaching wholesale suppliers. Bulk purchases – of florist's foam, for example – are more economical and you can usually find someone willing to split the goods and the cost with you. Try to keep your tools and other equipment in one place, close to where you work, so they are readily available.

For Cutting A good pair of secateurs, with precision ground stainless steel blades, is useful for harvesting and arranging. Secateurs with a double cutting edge – sometimes called parrot's peak or scissor action secateurs – are less likely to crush the material than anvil-type secateurs. Cleanly cut stems are easier to insert into florist's foam than crushed ones, and if you are cutting woody stems from garden shrubs, such as mahonia or magnolia, clean cuts are less likely to become diseased or die back. Long-handled pruning shears are useful for snipping branches from larch, beech, or other forest-size trees.

Good florist's scissors are expensive, but should last many years. In addition, they cut through ribbon and florist's wire, as well as stems, so you do not need to keep changing tools as you work. There are many styles and sizes available, some with pointed ends, others with round ends. Try the feel of several before buying, to find one that is well balanced, not too heavy, and comfortable to grip.

Sharp, stainless-steel knives are useful for cutting stems, large blocks of dried reindeer moss and blocks of florist's foam into various shapes. Sharpen knives and other cutting tools regularly, as dull edges do damage and also require more effort on your part to use.

If you dry your own flowers on a large scale, a leaf stripper, which removes thorns as well as foliage, is a useful and inexpensive gadget.

For Support Wire mesh, or chicken wire, has largely been replaced by florist's foam as the foundation for medium-sized and small dried flower displays. However, wire mesh has its advantages. Though you usually have to buy large lengths, it does work out cheaper than the equivalent amount of florist's foam, and is a more stable foundation for large-scale displays. Wire mesh can be wrapped round a single block of florist's foam to reinforce it, or wrapped around several pieces of florist's foam, as an outer, retaining skin. It is an excellent foundation for wreaths and swags, and can be shaped into a cone for dried flower 'trees'.

Wire mesh is also useful as a means of hanging flowers to dry (see pages 39-43), and it can be fixed to battens, then hung on a wall as a 'canvas' on which masses of dried flowers and foliage are fixed. Buy 13mm-5cm (½-2in) galvanized mesh, 30-90cm (1-3ft) wide, according to the size and delicacy of your dried material. Large-hole wire mesh is normally compacted into roughly double or triple thickness when used as support for stems. Compacted small-mesh netting is virtually impenetrable for large, thick stems, and is usually used stretched over the top and sides of florist's foam for additional support. If you use heavy gauge wire mesh, then wire cutters are necessary; for thinner gauge, secateurs or florist's scissors should suffice. Plastic-coated wire mesh is difficult to shape and crumple.

Grey or brown florist's foam for dried flowers is sold under various brand names. It is lightweight and theoretically re-usable, though it does tend to crumble with age, and becomes more and more perforated each time it is used. You can use the green, water-absorbent type normally used for fresh flowers, but it has a softer, denser consistency, and is more liable to disintegrate. Florist's foam is sold in square or rectangular blocks, in various sized cones, balls, rounded and oval wreath shapes. Polystyrene is less expensive than florist's foam, but has a tougher consistency and is harder to penetrate, so delicate stems often break when inserted.

Florist's foam should fit in a container as tightly as possible, to prevent it slipping or coming adrift from the florist's spikes (see below). You can often use the underside of the container as a template, to cut the florist's foam to the approximate shape. If it is slightly too big, you can shave it to fit, using a sharp knife. Pack small pieces of florist's foam round the inside edge of a container, to securely wedge the central piece, if necessary. Using several small pieces as a composite support is usually unsatisfactory, as they slip and break apart once stems are inserted.

Plastic florist's spikes, sometimes called frogs or flower prongs, come in various shapes, sizes and colours. (The colours are of no importance, as the spikes are never seen in the finished arrangement.) Florist's spikes are used to secure florist's foam to a container or other base. The spikes are fixed to the base with mastic. The spikes are inexpensive, but you can substitute several 13mm-2.5cm (½-1in) nails, depending on the size of the display, pushed pointed-side up, into a thick layer of mastic. Old-fashioned hairpins can also be used, or large, galvanized staples, pointed-ends up. Heavy metal pin-holders, such as those used for impaling fresh flowers, split dried florist's foam, and are not suitable.

On a small scale, mastic can be used as the support medium itself. A thick rope of mastic, for example, can be wrapped round the base of a candle stick, covered with a thin layer of sphagnum moss, then decorated with dried flowers. Mastic can also be used to fill miniature containers, into which sprigs of dried flowers are inserted. (Flowers with delicate stems should be wired up first.)

Split canes, 30-75cm (1-2½ft) long, are useful for lengthening the stems of flowers, or replacing weak stems altogether. Those left natural are less obtrusive than the green-dyed types.

Bamboo canes can discretely support whole bunches of flowers, to give height to the back of a large-scale arrangement.

For Adhesion and Tying As well as fixing spikes to bases, oil-based mastic, either the special green florist's mastic or the ordinary, all-purpose blue mastic, can fix sea shells, pieces of driftwood or pebbles to a flat base; or fix ribbons in place. Mastic can be used more than once, but it eventually loses its pliability and adhesive quality. Because mastic has a slightly sticky surface, bits and bobs of florist's foam, dust and dried material adhere to it, so store it completely enclosed. Mastic does not stick to a wet surface, and adheres better to non-porous, shiny surfaces than to porous or open-weave ones. White spirit can be used to clean mastic stuck to glazed surfaces.

Quick-drying transparent glue, such as a milk-based type, is useful for repair and decorative work. Use tooth-picks for applying glue to delicate, small-scale material. Rubbery adhesives are useful for sticking dried moss, lichen or raffia to bases or sides of containers.

String is useful for tying up bunches of flowers for drying. Buy three-or-four ply medium fillis, for strength and flexibility. If you use string in the construction of arrangements, natural jute fillis and raffia are less obtrusive visually than green or white fillis or polypropylene string. A large ball, reel or centre-draw spool is sensible, as small bits of string tend to disappear in the general mêlée. Whether or not you wire up dried flowers, florist's reel wire is useful for tying small bunches of dried flowers to the rims or handles of baskets, and for fixing wire netting to its container. Rubber bands, in several sizes, are also useful.

For Stability For top-heavy displays needing a firm, heavy base – tree-type arrangements in flower pots, for example – quick-setting plaster of Paris is useful and inexpensive. You can also use children's non-hardening modelling clay. Pebbles and larger stones are also good to counterbalance top-heavy displays, and, if attractive, can become part of the display itself. Sand is sometimes recommended, but it is messy to deal with and, like sugar, almost impossible to clean up completely. You can

also try dried pulses, such as kidney beans, haricots, lentils or split peas. Marbles are also useful and, for very large, lightweight containers, a brick inserted before the wire netting of florist's foam is fine.

For Wiring Even if you never wire up flowers in the traditional manner, you will find the following materials generally useful. As well as for such mundane tasks as mending broken stems, securing arrangements to their containers and tying up bunches for storage, wires are invaluable for constructing wreaths, garlands and Christmas tree ornaments.

Florist's wire comes on a reel or in cut lengths, called stub wires. Wires range in thickness, indicated either as the metric measurement of the diameter, or according to the older system of Standard Wire Gauge (SWG). Some labels give both measurements; with SWG, the lower the gauge number, the thicker the wire. In the metric system, higher numbers indicate thicker wires!

Rose wire, or silver reel wire, is tin-coated steel. The thinnest reel wire, it is available in two gauges and is useful for fixing wire netting into place, for wiring florets into tiny bunches, and for fixing floral decorations to hats, packages and so on. (At a pinch, use fuse wire instead.) Rose wire is also available in 15cm (6in) lengths. Annealed black reel wire is thicker, and useful for general work, such as tying stems into bunches. If only buying one reel, choose a medium gauge, such as 24SWG.

Annealed stub wires are sold in bundles. They range in length from 15-40cm (6-16in) and in gauge from 36-18 SWG. Professionals have a vast array, but for general purpose, a medium gauge, such as 22 or 24, is best. Stub wires can be easily cut in half or shortened, but short stub wires can't be lengthened, so go for a medium length, such as 23cm (9in). Stub wires can rust, so store in a dry place; it is convenient to store different lengths and gauges in separate containers.

Florist's tape, or gutta percha tape, gives a nice finish to a wired-up flower stem; creamy white, green or brown is more natural looking with dried flowers than pastel colours, such as pink and pale blue. Florist's tape is also useful for fixing wire netting to a container; and can be easily split in half lengthways for delicate work.

Useful Extras

Use dust sheets or plastic sheeting if your work area is carpeted or if you are handling large numbers of dried flowers, to keep cleaning up to a minimum. Spread the sheets out before you begin work, keeping in mind that dried material is very light and small pieces can end up some distance away from where they started. Equally sensible is a good supply of large-size rubbish bags and wire ties, to tidily dispose of the remains when you have finished. Dark-coloured plastic rubbish bags can also be cut up and used to line open-work containers, whether of woven wicker, bamboo, or Leeds ware-type china. This prevents the florist's foam or stems pushing through the gaps.

A tall-sided cardboard box, plastic bucket or small plastic dustbin is useful for keeping bunches of dried flowers or branches upright and in order while you work. Florists sometimes sell cheap, black plastic bucket-type containers; which are ideal for this purpose.

Definition of Terms

Alum A desiccant consisting of double sulphate of aluminium, usually combined with potassium.

Annealed Heated and allowed to cool slowly, to strengthen a material. Many types of florist's wires are annealed steel.

Annual A plant, such as love-in-a-mist, which completes its complete life cycle in one growing season; or a plant, such as tobacco plant, which is technically a tender perennial but grown as an annual in temperate climates.

Anther The part of the stamen that carries pollen.

Attar Essential fragrant oil, particularly from rose petals.

Biennial A plant, such as honesty, which takes two years to complete its life cycle, forming a rosette of leaves the first year and flowering and setting seed the second.

Borax A desiccant made of purified sodium borate, used in powder or crystal form.

Bract A modified leaf which surrounds a flower at its base, and can be the main decorative feature. Bells of Ireland and acanthus 'flowers' are showy bracts surrounding the tiny botanical flowers.

Calyx The outer, protective case of a bud or flower. A calyx can be green and leaf-like, as in the case of roses, or brightly coloured and petal-like, as in the case of fuchsias.

Clone One of a group of plants derived originally from a single plant, and propagated vegetatively. All clones have identical characteristics, which are in turn identical to those of the original parent.

Conditioning The process of preparing flowers, so they retain their freshness and beauty for the maximum amount of time.

Cultivar A cultivated variety, whether originally found in the wild, in gardens, or bred.

Desiccant A substance which absorbs moisture, especially as part of preservation.

Fasciation Flattened stems or branches, caused by the abnormal fusing together of several stems.

Floret An individual flower forming part of a compound flower or inflorescence. Chrysanthemums, daisies, dahlias and other members of the *Compositae* family have flowers composed of many florets.

Gall Swelling or distorted growth on leaves, stems, roots or branches, caused by bacteria, fungi, eelworms, mites or insects.

Genus A major division of a botanical family, sharing common structural characteristics, and subdivided into species.

Glycerine A sweet, clear liquid derived from fats, and use in the preservation of foliage.

Hybrid A plant resulting from crossing two different plants; F1 hybrids are the first generation resulting from a cross made between two pure-bred strains.

Inflorescence The flowering part of a plant, made up of individual florets.

Node A joint in the stem, from which new growth may occur.

Orris root The root of *Iris florentina* which is dried and ground for use in potpourris, pomanders, perfumes and medicine.

Panicle An elongated inflorescence, such as

lilac, with branched clusters of flowers along the stem.

Perennial A soft-stemmed plant that lives for more than two years, usually flowering annually. Herbaceous perennials, such as delphinium, die back to the ground each year. Evergreen perennials, such as Christmas rose, retain their foliage all year round.

Pollen The powder-like substance contained on the anther and which is the male element of fertilization.

Pomander A dried orange impregnated with spices or a ball of mixed spices used to scent a cupboard or closet.

Potpourri A mixture of fragrant dried petals, leaves, fixatives and essential oils, used to scent a room.

Raceme An elongated unbranched inflorescence, such as wisteria, made up of flowers on stalks along the central stem.

Raffia Fibre from the leaves of the palm *Raffia ruffia*, used as string or woven into mats, baskets or other goods.

Self flowers Flowers having a single colour, without additional markings.

Sepal One of the segments that make up a calyx.

Silica gel A desiccant, composed of silicon dioxide. Silica gel sometimes contains anhydrous cobalt (2) chloride, which acts as an indicator of the presence of water, appearing blue when dry and turning pale pink when wet.

Species A distinct group of naturally occurring plants, closely related to other species in its genus.

Spike An elongated inflorescence made up of stalkless or semi-stalked flowers.

Stamen The male part of a flower, made of a filament and anther. Closely packed stamens form the fluffy centres of many flowers.

Swag A festoon of flowers, usually hung on a wall or door.

Umbel An inflorescence, such as cow parsley or sea holly, in which the individual flower stalks grow from one point.

Whorl Three or more flowers growing in a ring around the stalk. Most of the *Labiatae* family, such as dead nettles, hyssop, phlomis, salvias and sages, have flowers growing in whorls.

INDEX

Numerals in *bold* refer to illustrations.

A

Abies forrestii 34
acanthus **24-5**, 100
achillea **20-1**, **22-3**, **28-9**, 32, 40, 42, **49**, 74, **82**, **91**, 100, 112, 118
acorns 36
acroclineum, *see* helipterum
Actinidia chinensis, *see* Chinese gooseberry
Aesculus, *see* horse chestnut
African marigolds 62, 124
agapanthus 16
air drying 31, 39-43, **40**, **41**, **42**, **43**
plants suitable for 33
alchemilla 112
alder 31, 55, 68-9, **82**, 91, 117
allium 63, 78, 100, 105
alyssum 124
America: eighteenth century flowers 53
American strawberry tree (*Euonymus americanus*) 65
ammobium **32**, 32, 60, 72, 112,117
anaphalis **20-1**, **28-9**, 32, **85**, **89**, 99, **113**
angelica 63, 110
Anigozanthus, *see* Kangaroo paw
animated oat (*Avena sterilis*) 63
annuals 60-4
clearing 33
planting out 98-9
sowing 63-4, 96-8, 124
thinning out 124
antifreeze: preservation in 121, 135-7
apple 48, 55, 65-6
apple of Peru (*Nicandra physalodes*) 63
Aquilegia, *see* columbine
arbutus 110
Arctium, *see* burdock
Armeria, *see* sea thrift
artemisia 36, 42, 76, 99
asparagus 100
aspidistra 42, 135, 137
astilbe **26-7**, 31, 42, 100
astrantia 100
aubergines 48, **49**
Aunt Eliza (*Curtonus paniculatus*) 100
Australian honeysuckle, *see* banksia

B

baby: gift for 87
Ballota pseudodictamnus 99
bamboo 91, 110, 128, 144
banksia 16, **17**, **20-1**, **24-5**, 91, 122, 144
bark 66, 70
barley **22-3**, **24-5**, 50, 128
bay 8, 78, 100-1
beachcombing 128-31
bedding plants 60
beech **26-7**, 55, 67, 76, 135, 148
beech mast 34
begonia 115
bell cups 16
bell jars 105, 115, **115**
bells of Ireland (*Moluccella laevis*) 32, 40, 42, 62, 63, 78, 91, 95
bergenia 99, 137
berries: drying 42
besom brooms 69
Bhutan pine (*Pinus wallichiana*) **34**
biennials 33, 124
birch 31, 55, 66, 67, 68-9, 81, 96, 110, 117
bird's nests 70
bistort 47, 127
bittersweet (*Celastrus orbiculatus*) 36, 53
black-eyed Susan, *see* rudbeckia
blackberry 112
blackthorn 70
blazing star (*Liatris* spp) 32, 100
bleaching wood 70
blessed thistle (*Silybum marianum*) 62
blue plants, buyer's guide 18-19
bluebell 31, **97**
bogwood 130
bonsai **119**
Bosnian pine (*Pinus leucodermis*) 34
bouquet 148
box 65, 67, 135
box elder (*Acer negundo violaceum*) 65
bracket fungi 38, **38**, **46**
branches:
bare 55
cleaning 70
wiring 73-4
bristlecone fir (*Abies bracteata*) 34
bristlecone pine (*Pinus aristata*) 34

broom bloom **20-1**, **24-5**, 47, **84**, 112, **119**, 122, **129**, **149**
broom stems 43, 67
brown plants, buyer's guide **26-7**
buddleia **26-7**, 144
bulrush 32, **32**, 37, 76, 91
bun moss (*Grimmia*) 104, 117
burdock 34, 39, 40
buttercups **97**
buttonwood 34

C

cabbage, ornamental 63
cabbage palm (*Sabal palmetto*) 17
calendula 124
camellia 135
camouflage 109
campanula **26-7**
campion 88, 100
canary grass **24-5**, **149**
Cape honey flower, *see* protea
Cape honeysuckle, *see* protea
caraway 63
cardoon 100
carline thistle (*Carlina vulgaris*) 37, 78, 127
Carpinus, *see* hornbeam
carrot (*Daucus*) 37, 63
cat-tail (*Typha latifolia*) 37
cedar 34
celastrum 53
celosia 40, 63
chamomile (*Anthemis* spp) **20-1**, 37, 47, 127
chanterelle (*Canterellus cibarius*) 38
cherry 65-6, 66, 110
chervil 63
chillis 78
Chinese gooseberry: stems 74
Chinese lanterns (*Physalis alkekengi*) 16, **22-3**, 40-2, **46**, **47**, 100
chives 18-19, 47
Choisya ternata 99, 135
Christmas 55
decorations 74, **82**, 83-4, **84-5**
tree, artificial 81, 83, **84-5**
cinnamon 78
Cissus antarctica 115
clary (*Salvia horminum*) 62
cleaning 104-5
clematis 16, **28-9**, 32, 36, 42, 67
climbers: pruning 64, 67
Clitocybe 38
clover (*Trilobium* spp) 127
cluster-flowered everlasting **22-3**, **113**
cockscomb (*Celosia argentea cristata*) 62, 124
collecting 127
Colonial style arrangement 52-3, **52**
columbine (*Aquilegia*) 74, 100

common laurel (*Prunus laurocerasus*) 99, 136
cone trees 80-1, **80**, **81**
cones 34, 55, **66-7**, 76, 78, **84**
wiring 73, **73**
conifer 'ropes' 110
conservation 70, 131
containers 56-9, **57**, **58**, **59**
Colonial style 53
colours 56-8
for indoor gardens 117
making 108-9
materials 58, 59
miniature 118
size 59
Victorian 115
coral 128, **131**
coral-bark maple (*Acer palmatum* 'Senkaki') 65
coriander 63
cork oak bark **49**, **66-7**
corn 128
cornflower (*Centaurea cyanus*) 16, **18-19**, 31, 62, 108, 124, 127, 146
Cortaderia, *see* pampas grass
cotoneaster 135, 136
cotton lavender 40
cotton plant (*Gossypium herbaceum*) 112
cotton thistle (*Onopordon acanthium*) 127
country casual arrangements 144-6, **145**
cow parsley **26-7**, 37, 53, 63, **85**, 148
crab-apple **20-1**, 48, **49**
cranesbill **26-7**
craspedia 91, 112
Crataegus, *see* hawthorn
cream plants, buyer's guide **28-9**
crocosmia 37, 118
cryptomeria 34, 55
cucumber 78
cucumber vine (*Echinocystis lobata*) 63
cupid's dart (*Catananche caerulea*) 60
cupressus 34
currants: prunings 66
cycas palm, *see* sago palm
Cynara, *see* cardoon
Cyperus alternifolius 128
cypress: leaves 148
cypress knees 130

D

dahlia 74, 122, 124
daisies 37, **97**, **116**
date palm (*Phoenix* spp) 17
decoy ducks **50-1**
definitions of terms 152-3
delphinium **125**
buds 109
flowers 47, 62, 100, 112, 117, 118, 122

delphinium, *cont.*
hanging 40
picking 31
staking 124
stems 74
storing 43
wiring 108
deodar cedar 34
desiccants:
flowers to dry in 134
preserving in 31, 132-4, **133**
types 132
dill 63
dock (sorrel) (*Rumex acetosa*) **26-7**, 32, 37, 53, 100
dogwood (*Cornus* spp) 55, 65
doll's house furniture **86**, 87
Douglas fir (*Pseudotsuga menziesii*) 34
driftwood 59, 91, 130
dryandra 16, 122
dyes 14, 95

E

Easter arrangements 112-13, **112-13**
echinops **18-19**, **28-9**, 76, 78, **90**, 100, **107**
Edgeworthia papyrifera 67
eggs **113**, 114
elaeagnus **22-3**, 67, 99, 110, 135
Eleocharis acicularis, *see* hair grass
elm 65
epergnes 51
Epilobium, *see* rose bay willowherb
equipment 150-2
escallonia 65, 135, 136
eucalyptus 43, 47, 67, 95, 117, 122, 135
bark 66
seed pods 16
Euonymus alatus 65
evening primrose **26-7**
everlasting daisy 60
exotics 16, **17**

F

fabric 109
false indigo (*Baptisia australis*) 32, 100
fan palm (*Chamaerops humilis*) 16
Fatsia japonica 135, 136, 137
feather flower **22-3**
feathers 37, **82**
fennel 63, 131, 144
fern palm, *see* sago palm
ferns **24-5**, 115, 148
feverfew (*Chrysanthemum parthenium*) 32, 37, 127
filberts 51
fir (*Abies* spp and cvs) 34
fixatives 138
florists 14, 122
flowers: buying for drying 122

foliage 109
drying 42
plants for 99
preservation 135-7, **136**
storing 43
wiring 73-4
formal flower arrangements 44, **45**, 47
Forsythia × intermedia 'Spectabilis' 65
foxglove (Digitalis purpurea) 26-7, 37, 100, 124, **127**
foxglove tree (Paulownia tomentosa) 36
fritillary 31
fruit 51
fungi 38, **38**

G

galax 91, 122, 128, **129**
game, mock **50-1**, 51
game feathers 37
Ganoderma 38
garlands 110-11, **111**
garlic **8**
gas plant (Dictamnus albus) 100
Georgian Colonial style 53
Geranium, see cranesbill
giant thistle (Onopordum acanthium) 62
gift wrapping 76-8, **77**
gifts **86**, 87-8, **88**
glass domes 105, 115, **115**
gleditsia 36
glixia **22-3**, 78, 83, 118, 144
globe amaranth (Gomphrena globosa) **18-19**, 62, 88
globe artichokes 100, **101**
globes 80-1, **80, 81**
glycerine: preserving in 31, 42, 99, 121, 135-7, **136**
foliage suitable for 137
goldenrod 53, 74, 100, 112, 127
gomphrena 40, 60
gorse 70
gourds (Lagenaria spp) 48, **48, 49**, 63
as containers 109-110
grain **46**, 48, **49**, 50
grape hyacinth **28-9**, 31, 32, 100
grape vines 42, 67, 130
grasses **50-1**, 53, 58, 62, 76, **106**, 127-8, 144
drying 42
harvesting **126**, 128
ripeness 14
seeds 63
stems 74
storing 43
wiring 73
green plants, buyer's guide **24-5**
Griselinia littoralis 65, 135
ground elder 37
growers 14

gypsophila **28-9**, 76, 78, 81, **89**, 100, 112, 118, 122, **149**
bundling 72, 108
as filler 47
handling 39
massed 58, 91
stems 117

H

hair grass **18-19, 20-1, 28-9, 80, 149**
Hakea 16, **17, 24-5**
Hallowe'en display **49**
handling dried flowers 39
hare's tail grass (Lagurus ovatus) **24-5, 28-9**, 62, **85**, 88, **107**, 112
haricots 51
Harry Lauder's walking stick (Corylus avellana 'Contorta') 65
harvest arrangements **46**, 47-8, 47-51
harvesting 31, 32-3
hats: decorating 106-8, **106-7, 198**
hawthorn 48, **49**, 70, 112
hazel (Corylus spp) **66-7**
catkins 31, 68-9
contorted (C. avellana 'Contorta') 65
nuts 36, 51
stems 55, 68-9, 81, 91, 96, 117
heather **18-19**, 42, **66-7**, 67, 70
hedges: pruning 65
helichrysum 14, **18-19, 20-1, 22-3, 50-1, 80**, 88, **91, 106**, 112, **113**, 122, 124
foliage 42
wiring 40, 71, **71**, 72
Helipterum (sunray) **20-1, 22-3**, 40, 60, **62-9**, 96-8, 108, 112, **113, 116**, 117, 124
hellebore (Helleborus spp) 101, **133**, 135
hemlock 34
herb sachets **8**
herbaceous perennials 31
herbs 63, 100-1, 148
in wreath or swag 76
hogweed (Heracleum sphondylium) 37, **68**, 81, 110
holiday trophies 130-1
hollyhocks (Althaea spp and cvs) 31, 52, 62, 100, 124
honesty **28-9**, 39-43, 112
honeysuckle (Lonicera spp) 67
hops (Humulus lupulus) 36, **36**, 42, 127
horehound (Marrubium vulgare) 99
horn of plenty (Craterellus cornucopioides) 38
hornbeam 37
horse chestnut 34-6
hosta **28-9**, 42, 43, 99-100, 137
house-warming present 87
hyacinth 93, 138

hydrangea 13, 16, **18-19, 20-1, 30**, 42, **50-1**, 78, **85, 89**, 118, 127
fresh 31

I

immortelles 32, 39-43, 60, 93
imports 130-1
Indian bean tree (Catalpa bignonioides) 36
Indian maize 50
indoor dried garden **116**, 117
insects: deterring 36, 43
Iris **26-7**, 100
foetidissima 100
sibirica 74
ivy (Hedera spp) 68, **69**, 69-70, 115, 118
aerial roots 69-70
bark 70
fresh 110
preserving 135, 137

J

jacaranda 16
Japanese bitter orange (Poncirus trifoliata) 65
Jerusalem sage 112
Jew's ear (Auricularia auricula) 38
Jew's mallow (Kerria japonica) 65
Job's tears (Coix lacryma-jobi) 62-3
Judas tree 36

K

kale, ornamental 63
kangaroo paw **17, 22-3**
knapweed (Centaurea: Cirsium, Carduus spp) **18-19**, 100, 127
knotweed 127
Korean fir (Abies Koreana) **35**
kumquats **49**

L

lady's mantle (Alchemilla mollis) 31, 42, 47, 91, 99, 100, 108, 122, 148
lamb's tongue (Stachys lanata) 42, 99
larch 34, 55, **66-7**, 69, **84**
large-scale displays 142-4, **143**
Larix, see larch
larkspur (Consolida regalis) **18-19, 20-1**, 31, 62, 72, **89, 107**, 109, 118, **125**
laurel 67, 109, 135
lavender (Lavandula spp) 42, 78, 138, **141**, 148
potpourri recipe 140
lawn 117
leaves, see foliage
leek **28-9**, 42, 63, **85**, 105
lemon potpourri 140
lenten rose (Helleborus orientalis) **133**

lentils 51
leopard's bane (Doronicum pardalianches) 127
Leucobryum glaucum 102-4
Leucodendron 16, 122
liatris 32
lichen 70, 102
lily 122
liverworts 102
lollipop tree 80, **80**, 142
love-in-a-mist (Nigella damascena) **18-19**, 33, **49**, 59, 60, 62, 78, 96-8, 124
love-lies-bleeding (Amaranthus caudatus, A. hybridus) **24-5**, 32, 62, 74, 91, 98-9
lupin, 100, 124

M

magnolia 36, 42, 67, 109, 135
mahonia 67, 135, 137
mail order 17
maize **22-3**, 46, 76
mallow (Lavatera spp and cvs) 62, **141**
manzanita 70, 112
maple (Acer spp) 37, 110
coral-bark (A. palmatum 'Senkaki') 65
field (A. campestre) 65
snake-bark 66
marble galls 70
marigolds 53
mauve plants, buyer's guide **18-19**
mayweed (Matricaria recutitia) 127
Mexican orange blossom (Choisya ternata) 99, 135
mice 40
Milium, see millet
milkweed (Asclepias tuberosa) 32, 36, 37, 96
millet 17, 50, 128
mimosa **17**, 36, 40, 42, 112, 122
miniatures 118, **119**
mint (Mentha spp) **18-19**, 127
mitsumata (Edgeworthia papyrifera) 67
modern arrangements 91
monkey puzzle (Araucaria araucana) 42, 76
montbretia (Crocosmia) **26-7**, 100
moss 102-4, **103**, 117
mugwort (Artemisia vulgaris) **18-19**, 127
mulberry (Morus) 66
mullein (Verbascum spp) 37, 40, 124
mushrooms **8**, 38

N

narcissus 138
nests 70, 114

nipplewort (Lapsana communis) 37, 47, 76, 81
noble fir (Abies procera) 34
nuts 51, 76, **82**
wiring 73, **73**

O

oak 55, **119**
oak galls **66-7**, 70
oat grass **149**
oats (Avena) 50, 128
animated (A. sterilis) 63
wild (A. fatua) 128
Oenothera, see evening primrose
old man's beard (Clematis vitalba) 36, 42
onions 63
Onopordum **36**
orange plants, buyer's guide **22-3**
oriental styles 44
Orthotrichum diaphanum 104
ox-eye daisy (Leucanthemum vulgare) 127
oyster fungus (Pleurotus ostreatus) 38

P

paeony 31, 52, 100, 101, 124
paints 96
palmeto palm, see cabbage palm
palms 16
pampas grass 16, **28-9**, 32
papyrus (Cyperus papyrus) 128
parsley **8**, 63
pasque flower 32
pearl everlasting (Anaphalis spp) 99
pears 48, 65-6
pebbles 129-30
Peruvian lily 122
Phlaris canariensis, see canary grass
phlomis (see also Jerusalem sage) 32
pine 34, 55
pink plants, buyer's guide **20-1**
plane 34, 66, **66-7**
plantain **26-7**
Platanus occidentalis, see buttonwood
planting 101
plum 65-6
polyanthus 93
polygonum **116**
polysticus bracket fungus (Trametes versicolor) 38, **38**
pomanders 79, **79**
Poncirus trifoliata 112
poppy **26-7**, 98, 109
opium (Papaver somniferum) 62, 74
seed heads 91, 100, 128, **129**
Portugal laurel (Prunus lusitanica) 99, 110
posies **146**, 147-8, **147**

potpourri 78, 83, **86**, 87, 138-41, **139**
  flowers suitable for 141
  recipes 140
primrose 93
Prince of Wales's feathers (*Celosia argentea plumosa*) 33, 60, 62, 124
privet 135
protea 16, 17, **22-3**, 42, **91**, 91, 122, 144
prunings 64
Prunus laurocerasus 99, 136
pulses 51
pumpkin 48, **49**
Puritan arrangement 52-3
pussy willow 31, 67

Q

quaking grass (*Briza media*) **24-5**, **49**, 63, **63**, 88, 112, 118, 128, **149**
Queen Anne's lace, *see* cow parsley

R

rabbit's tail grass, *see* hare's tail grass
raffia 95
rat's-tail statice (*Statice suworowii*) 32, 63
rattan palm (*Calamus* spp) 17
red plants, buyer's guide **20-1**
redshank 127
redwood 34
reed sweet grass 128
reindeer moss (*Cladonia rangiferina*) 88, 102, 104
repairs 105
Rhodanthe manglesii, *see* Swan River everlasting
rhododendron 109
rhubarb 100
ribbons **94**, 95
rigid bulrush (*Typha latifolia*) 37
ripeness: checking 14
robinia 36, 142
roots 70

rose **20-1**, **22-3**, 39, 47, 52, 88, **89**, 108, 138, **141**, **149**
  hips **20-1**
  potpourri recipe 140
  preservation **133**
  wiring 72, **72**
rose bay willowherb **18-19**
rosemary 78, 101, 148
Rubus cockburnianus 65
rudbeckia **26-7**, 32, 47, 53, 62
rushes 128
rye 128

S

safflower (*Carthamus tinctorius*) **24-5**, 60, 84, **89**
sage (*Salvia officinalis*) 100, 148
sago palm (*Cycas revoluta*) 16, 76
St John's wort (*Hypericum*) 100
samphire 131
sand flower, *see* ammobium
Santolina chamaecyparissus, *see* cotton lavender
scabious **26-7**, 78, 124
sea buckthorn (*Hippophae rhamnoides*) 70, 112
sea holly (*Eryngium* spp) **18-19**, 39-43, 100, **130**, 144, 131, **131**
sea lavender (*Limonium* spp) **28-9**, 47, **50-1**, 53, **80**, 81, 118, 131, **131**, 144
sea thrift 100
sea wormwood (*Artemisia maritima*) 127
seakale 144
sedges 128
sedum **26-7**, 99, 100
seed: germination **64**
seed: obtaining 63
seed heads 100
  storing 43
seed pods 16, 31, 34-7, **49**, 76
  drying 42
  picking 32
selaginella 104
senecio 42
shells 128, **129**, 131

Shirley poppy 124
shoo-fly plant (*Nicandra physalodes*) 63
shops: displays 14, **15**
shrubs: pruning 64-5
silica gel preserved material 39, 43
silver strawberry (*Leptospermum* spp) 122
sneezewort (*Achillea ptarmica*) 127
snowberry (*Symphoricarpos*) 100
Sorbus, *see* whitebeam
sorrel (*Rumex acetosa*) **26-7**, 32, 37, 53, 100
sphagnum moss (*Sphagnum* spp) 102, 117
spiders' webs 104-5
spindle tree (*Euonymus europeus*) 65
spiraea **20-1**
spotted laurel (*Aucuba japonica*) 99
spruce 34
squashes **49**
squirrel's tail grass (*Hordeum jubatum*) 62
staking 124
statice (*Limonium* spp) 14, **18-19**, **22-3**, **28-9**, 32, **50-1**, 60, 63, 100, 112, 118
stems:
  disguising 47
  handling 39
  sections 110
  shaping 43
stirlingia 17, **18-19**, 91
storing 43
strawflower, *see* helichrysum
sugar pine (*Pinus lambertiana*) 34
sumach (*Rhus typhina*) 36, 47, 53
sunflower, annual (*Helianthus annuus*) 62, 98
sunlight 14, 40
sunray (*Helipterum*) **20-1**, **22-3**, **28-9**, 40, 60, 96-8, 108, 112, **113**, **116**, 117, 124
swags 74-6, **111**

Swan River everlasting (*Helipterum manglesii*) **20-1**, 60
sweet chestnut (*Castanea*) **26-7**, 34-6, **46**, 51, **66-7**
sweet galingale (*Cyperus longus*) 128
sweet gum (*Liquidambar styraciflua*) 65
sweet sultan (*Centaurea moschata*) 62
sweet William **18-19**, **20-1**, 124
sweetmeats 51
sycamore 37

T

Tagetes, *see* African marigold
tansy (*Tanacetum vulgare*) **22-3**, 32, 37, 53, 100, 131
tassel flower, *see* love-lies-bleeding
teasel (*Dipsacus fullonum*) **26-7**, 37, 39, 53, 63, 76, 78, 146
techniques 39-43
terms 152-3
terrariums 117
thistles 32, **36**, 37, **50-1**, 60-2, 127
thorn 65
thuja 34
timothy grass **24-5**, **28-9**, **116**
tips 152
tools 150-2
tree of heaven (*Ailanthus glandulosa*) 36
tree trunks 66
trees 65-7
  pruning 64
tulip 31, 100
Turk's cap gourd **49**
tussy mussies 148

V

Valentine's Day presents 88, **88**, **89**
vanilla beans 78
varnish 96
vegetables 100-1

velvet flower, *see* love-lies-bleeding
veronica 100
Victorian arrangements 114-15, **115**

W

wallflowers 138
Wardian cases 117
water plantain (*Alisma plantago aquatica*) 81
watering 101
western styles 44
wheat **22-3**, 50
white plants, buyer's guide **28-9**, 112
whitebeam (*Sorbus*) 137
willow (*Salix* spp) 43, 55, **64**, 65, 67
  contorted (curly) (*S. matsudana* 'Tortuosa') 65, **65**, **66-7**, **90**, 91
willow myrtle **22-3**
winged everlasting, *see* ammobium
wiring 71-3, **71**, **72**, **73**
wisteria 36, 67, 70
wood:
  bleaching 70
  cleaning 70
woody pear (*Xylomelum angustifolium*) 16
wormwood (*Artemisia absinthum*) 127
wreaths 74, **75**, **82**

X

xeranthemum **18-19**, **28-9**, 60, **107**, **131**

Y

yarrow (*Achillea millefolium*) 37, 53, **113**, 127
yellow plants, buyer's guide **22-3**, 112
yew 70

Z

zinnia 62

Acknowledgements

The author would like to thank the following people and suppliers:
The Alderney Pottery
Anne Bearn
Durleighmarsh Farm
Jessica Lawrence
Diana Mellor
W. Morgan & Sons, Petersfield

Marshall Cavendish Books Ltd. would like to thank **Moyses Stevens**, 6 Bruton Street, London W1, for providing some material for photographic sessions.

Picture credits

Chattels, 53 Chalk Farm Road, NW1: 15. *Aubrey Dewar:* 114(r). *Ray Duns:* 71, 72, 73, 74, 75, 79, 80, 104, 108, 111, 133, 136/7, 139, 147. *Valerie Finnis:* 130. *Ranald Mackechnie:* 59. *S & O Mathews:* 12/3, 40, 41, 54/5, 68, 81, 92/3, 120/1, 126. *Roger Phillips:* endpapers, 4, 8/9, 11, 16/7, 18/9, 20/1, 22/3, 24/5, 26/7, 28/9, 38(r), 44/5, 46/7, 48/9, 52, 57, 66/7, 77, 82/3, 84/5, 86, 88, 89, 90, 94, 106/7, 112/3, 116, 119, 131, 140/1, 142/3, 145, 148/9. *Peter Reilly:* 6, 58. *Kim Sayer:* 42. *Harry Smith Collection:* 30, 34, 35, 36(1) Polunin Collection, 36(r) Polunin Collection, 38(1), 43, 64, 69 Polunin Collection, 97, 100, 102, 103, 134, *Michael Warren:* 32(br), 47, 48, 61, 63, 65, 101, 124, 125, 127.